The Millennium Development Goals Report 2010

UNITED NATIONS

NEW YORK, 2010

WE CAN
END POVERTY
2015 MILLENNIUM
DEVELOPMENT
GOALS

NOLOAN
PER
UNI
ST/ESA
m34

Foreword

The Millennium Declaration in 2000 was a milestone in international cooperation, inspiring development efforts that have improved the lives of hundreds of millions of people around the world. Ten years later, world leaders will gather again at the United Nations in New York to review progress, assess obstacles and gaps, and agree on concrete strategies and actions to meet the eight Millennium Development Goals by 2015.

The Goals represent human needs and basic rights that every individual around the world should be able to enjoy—freedom from extreme poverty and hunger; quality education, productive and decent employment, good health and shelter; the right of women to give birth without risking their lives; and a world where environmental sustainability is a priority, and women and men live in equality. Leaders also pledged to forge a wide-ranging global partnership for development to achieve these universal objectives.

This report shows how much progress has been made. Perhaps most important, it shows that the Goals are achievable when nationally owned development strategies, policies and programmes are supported by international development partners. At the same time, it is clear that improvements in the lives of the poor have been unacceptably slow, and some hard-won gains are being eroded by the climate, food and economic crises.

The world possesses the resources and knowledge to ensure that even the poorest countries, and others held back by disease, geographic isolation or civil strife, can be empowered to achieve the MDGs.

Meeting the goals is everyone's business. Falling short would multiply the dangers of our world – from instability to epidemic diseases to environmental degradation. But achieving the goals will put us on a fast track to a world that is more stable, more just, and more secure.

Billions of people are looking to the international community to realize the great vision embodied in the Millennium Declaration. Let us keep that promise.

BAN KI-MOON
Secretary-General, United Nations

Overview

Keeping the promise

Five years from the target date for the Millennium Development Goals, leaders from around the world will be gathering at the United Nations to undertake a comprehensive review of progress and together chart a course for accelerated action on the MDGs between now and 2015.

Many countries are moving forward, including some of the poorest, demonstrating that setting bold, collective goals in the fight against poverty yields results. For every life that has benefited from the establishment of a quantitative, time-bound framework of accountability, the MDGs have made a real difference.

But unmet commitments, inadequate resources, lack of focus and accountability, and insufficient dedication to sustainable development have created shortfalls in many areas. Some of these shortfalls were aggravated by the global food and economic and financial crises.

Nevertheless, the data and analysis on the following pages provide clear evidence that targeted interventions, sustained by adequate funding and political commitment, have resulted in rapid progress in some areas. In others, the poorest groups, those without education or living in more remote areas, have been neglected and not provided the conditions to improve their lives.

Building on successes

The collective efforts towards achievement of the MDGs have made inroads in many areas. Encouraging trends before 2008 had put many regions on track to achieve at least some of the goals. The economic growth momentum in developing regions remains strong and, learning from the many successes of even the most challenged countries, achieving the MDGs is still within our grasp:

- Progress on poverty reduction is still being made, despite significant setbacks due to the 2008-2009 economic downturn, and food and energy crises. The developing world as a whole remains on track to achieve the poverty reduction target by 2015. The overall poverty rate is still expected to fall to 15 per cent by 2015, which translates to around 920 million people living under the international poverty line—half the number in 1990.

- Major advances have been made in getting children into school in many of the poorest countries, most of them in sub-Saharan Africa.

- Remarkable improvements in key interventions—for malaria and HIV control, and measles immunization, for example—have cut child deaths from 12.5 million in 1990 to 8.8 million in 2008.

- Between 2003 and 2008, the number of people receiving antiretroviral therapy increased tenfold—from 400,000 to 4 million—corresponding to 42 per cent of the 8.8 million people who needed treatment for HIV.

- Major increases in funding and a stronger commitment to control malaria have accelerated delivery of malaria interventions. Across Africa, more communities are benefiting from bed net protection and more children are being treated with effective drugs.

- The rate of deforestation, though still alarmingly high, appears to have slowed, due to tree-planting schemes combined with the natural expansion of forests.

- Increased use of improved water sources in rural areas has narrowed the large gap with urban areas, where coverage has remained at 94 per cent—almost unchanged since 1990. However, the safety of water supplies remains a challenge and urgently needs to be addressed.

- Mobile telephony continues to expand in the developing world and is increasingly being used for m-banking, disaster management and other non-voice applications for development. By the end of 2009, cellular subscriptions per 100 people had reached the 50 per cent mark.

Bridging the gaps

Though progress has been made, it is uneven. And without a major push forward, many of the MDG targets are likely to be missed in most regions. Old and new challenges threaten to further slow progress in some areas or even undo successes achieved so far.

The most severe impact of climate change is being felt by vulnerable populations who have contributed least to the problem. The risk of death or disability and economic loss due to natural disasters is increasing globally and is concentrated in poorer countries. Armed conflict remains a major threat to human security and to hard-won MDG gains. Large populations of refugees remain in camps with limited opportunities to improve their lives. In 2009, 42 million people had been displaced by conflict or persecution, four fifths of them in developing countries.

The number of people who are undernourished has continued to grow, while slow progress in reducing the prevalence of hunger stalled—or even reversed itself—in some regions between 2000-2002 and 2005-2007. About one in four children under the age of five are underweight, mainly due to lack of food and quality food, inadequate water, sanitation and health services, and poor care and feeding practices.

An estimated 1.4 billion people were still living in extreme poverty in 2005. Moreover, the effects of the global financial crisis are likely to persist: poverty rates will be slightly higher in 2015 and even beyond, to 2020, than they would have been had the world economy grown steadily at its pre-crisis pace.

Gender equality and the empowerment of women are at the heart of the MDGs and are preconditions for overcoming poverty, hunger and disease. But progress has been sluggish on all fronts—from education to access to political decision-making.

Achieving the MDGs will also require increased attention to those most vulnerable. Policies and interventions will be needed to eliminate the persistent or even increasing inequalities between the rich and the poor, between those living in rural or remote areas or in slums versus better-off urban populations, and those disadvantaged by geographic location, sex, age, disability or ethnicity:

- In all developing regions, children in rural areas are more likely to be underweight than urban children. In Latin America and the Caribbean and parts of Asia, this disparity increased between 1990 and 2008.

- The gap between the richest and the poorest households remains enormous. In Southern Asia, 60 per cent of children in the poorest areas are underweight compared to 25 per cent of children in the richest households.

- In developing regions overall, girls in the poorest 20 per cent of households are 3.5 times more likely to be out of school than girls in the richest households and four times more likely to be out of school than boys from the richest households.

- Even in countries close to achieving universal primary education, children with disabilities are the majority of those excluded.

- Maternal health is one of the areas in which the gap between rich and poor is most conspicuous. While almost all births are attended by skilled health personnel in the developed countries, less than half of women receive such care when giving birth in parts of the developing world.

- Disparities in access to care during pregnancy are also striking, with women in the richest households 1.7 times more likely to visit a skilled health worker at least once before birth than the poorest women.

- Lack of education is another major obstacle to accessing tools that could improve people's lives. For instance, poverty and unequal access to schooling perpetuate high adolescent birth rates, jeopardizing the health of girls and diminishing their opportunities for social and economic advancement.

- Contraceptive use is four times higher among women with a secondary education than among those with no education. For women in the poorest households and among those with no education, negligible progress was seen over the last decade.

- Only about half of the developing world's population are using improved sanitation, and addressing this inequality will have a major impact on several of the MDGs. Disparities between rural and urban areas remain daunting, with only 40 per cent of rural populations covered. And while 77 per cent of the population in the richest 20 per cent of households use improved sanitation facilities, the share is only 16 per cent of those in the poorest households.

Towards 2015

The Millennium Declaration represents the most important promise ever made to the world's most vulnerable people. The MDG framework for accountability derived from the Declaration has generated an unprecedented level of commitment and partnership in building decent, healthier lives for billions of people and in creating an environment that contributes to peace and security.

The Millennium Development Goals are still attainable. The critical question today is how to transform the pace of change from what we have seen over the last decade into dramatically faster progress. The experience of these last ten years offers ample evidence of what works and has provided tools that can help us achieve the MDGs by 2015. The Millennium Development Goals summit in September will be an opportunity for world leaders to translate this evidence into a concrete agenda for action.

SHA ZUKANG
Under-Secretary-General for Economic and Social Affairs

Goal 1

Eradicate extreme poverty and hunger

TARGET
Halve, between 1990 and 2015, the proportion of people whose income is less than $1 a day

The global economic crisis has slowed progress, but the world is still on track to meet the poverty reduction target

Proportion of people living on less than $1.25 a day, 1990 and 2005 (Percentage)

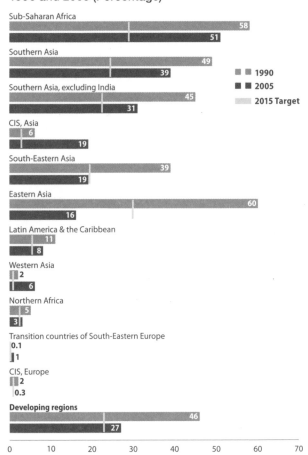

Sub-Saharan Africa — 58 / 51

Southern Asia — 49 / 39

Southern Asia, excluding India — 45 / 31

CIS, Asia — 6 / 19

South-Eastern Asia — 39 / 19

Eastern Asia — 60 / 16

Latin America & the Caribbean — 11 / 8

Western Asia — 2 / 6

Northern Africa — 5 / 3

Transition countries of South-Eastern Europe — 0.1 / 1

CIS, Europe — 2 / 0.3

Developing regions — 46 / 27

- ■ ■ 1990
- ■ ■ 2005
- 2015 Target

Robust growth in the first half of the decade reduced the number of people in developing regions living on less than $1.25 a day from 1.8 billion in 1990 to 1.4 billion in 2005, while the poverty rate dropped from 46 per cent to 27 per cent. The global economic and financial crisis, which began in the advanced economies of North America and Europe in 2008, sparked abrupt declines in exports and commodity prices and reduced trade and investment, slowing growth in developing countries. Nevertheless, the momentum of economic growth in developing countries is strong enough to sustain progress on the poverty reduction target. The overall poverty rate is still expected to fall to 15 per cent by

2015, indicating that the Millennium Development Goal (MDG) target can be met. This translates into around 920 million people living under the international poverty line—half the number in 1990.

Newly updated estimates from the World Bank suggest that the crisis will leave an additional 50 million people in extreme poverty in 2009 and some 64 million by the end of 2010 relative to a no-crisis scenario, principally in sub-Saharan Africa and Eastern and South-Eastern Asia. Moreover, the effects of the crisis are likely to persist: poverty rates will be slightly higher in 2015 and even beyond, to 2020, than they would have been had the world economy grown steadily at its pre-crisis pace.

The fastest growth and sharpest reductions in poverty continue to be recorded in Eastern Asia. Poverty rates in China are expected to fall to around 5 per cent by 2015. India, too, has contributed to the large reduction in global poverty. Measured at the $1.25 a day poverty line, poverty rates there are expected to fall from 51 per cent in 1990 to 24 per cent in 2015, and the number of people living in extreme poverty will likely decrease by 188 million. All developing regions except sub-Saharan Africa, Western Asia and parts of Eastern Europe and Central Asia are expected to achieve the MDG target. These shortfalls reflect slow growth in sub-Saharan Africa in the 1990s and the transition from planned to market economies that saw poverty increase, albeit from very low levels, in some countries of Eastern Europe and the former Soviet Union.

The lack of good quality surveys carried out at regular intervals and delays in reporting survey results continue to hamper the monitoring of poverty. Gaps are particularly acute in sub-Saharan Africa, where more than half of countries lack sufficient data to make comparisons over the full range of the MDGs, and among small island states in the Pacific and the Caribbean. Surveys deliver important information—not just in the change in average income or consumption, but also in its distribution. This year's poverty estimates integrate 31 new household surveys. Combining these new surveys with last year's growth forecast suggests a 0.5 percentage point decline (after taking into account the effect of the financial crisis) in the aggregate poverty headcount index in 2015—from 15.5 per cent to 15.0 per cent. Only with more timely data can accurate reports on progress towards the MDGs be provided.

Prior to the crisis, the depth of poverty had diminished in almost every region

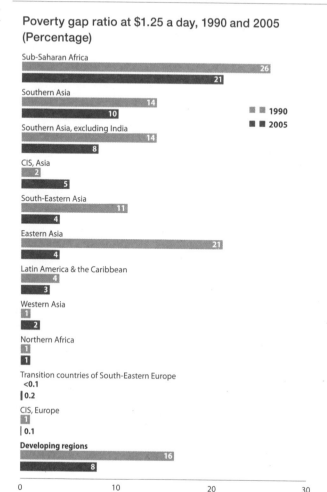

Poverty gap ratio at $1.25 a day, 1990 and 2005 (Percentage)

The poverty gap measures the shortfall in incomes of people living below the poverty line. While the international poverty line is set at a level typical of very poor countries, many people live on even less than that amount. Economic growth and improvements in the distribution of income or consumption reduce the depth of poverty. Since 1990, the depth of poverty has decreased in all regions except Western Asia. In 2005, the average income of people living below the poverty line stood at $0.88. The depth of poverty was greatest in sub-Saharan Africa, but has fallen since 1999 to reach the level of Eastern Asia in 1990.

Investments in disaster risk reduction can yield long-term benefits, including progress on the MDGs

The risk of death or disability and economic loss resulting from natural disasters is increasing globally and is concentrated in poorer countries. Reducing such risk can have multiplier effects that can accelerate achievement of the MDGs. The horrific loss of life from earthquakes in Haiti, Chile and China, and floods in Brazil, underscore the need to make the built environment more resilient in the face of potential hazards—both seismic and climatic (or weather-related).

Urbanization, climate change and ecosystem degradation are increasing the toll of natural disasters, and countries least able to reduce their risk are suffering the most. An estimated 97 per cent of global mortality risk from natural disasters is faced by populations in low- and lower-middle-income countries, which also experience higher economic losses relative to the size of their economies. From the start of 2008 through March 2010, 470,000 people were reportedly killed as a result of natural disasters; economic losses were estimated to be more than $262 billion (not including 2010). Small island developing states and landlocked developing countries together constitute 60 per cent and 67 per cent, respectively, of the countries considered to have a high or very high economic vulnerability to natural hazards.

Experience from countries has shown that investments in disaster risk reduction produce long-term benefits—from reduced future losses and avoided reconstruction to co-benefits such as more robust livelihoods, resilient communities, and protective and productive ecosystems. In Peru, incorporation of risk reduction into development has led to benefits that exceeded costs by as much as 37 times. When China spent $3.15 billion on reducing the impact of floods between 1960 and 2000, it averted losses estimated at $12 billion.

TARGET
Achieve, full and productive employment and decent work for all, including women and young people

Deterioration of the labour market, triggered by the economic crisis, has resulted in a decline in employment

Employment-to-population ratio, 1998, 2008 and 2009 preliminary estimates

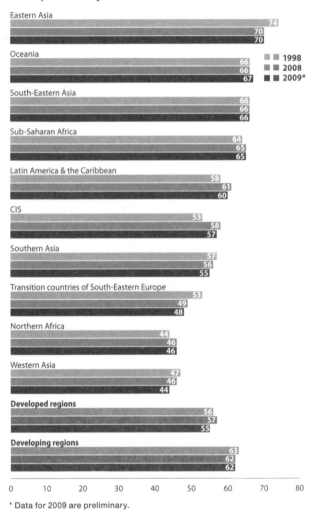

* Data for 2009 are preliminary.

The bursting of the housing bubble in the United States in 2007 and subsequent paralysis of the global financial system became an economic and labour market crisis that plagued the world throughout 2009. The cascading crisis crippled economies, reduced enterprise capacities and forced millions of people out of work. Many workers resorted to vulnerable forms of employment as the ranks of the working poor swell.

As the crisis deepened, government stimulus measures began to curb the slide in economic activity and lessen the impact of global job losses. The coordinated efforts of countries responding to the crisis have been instrumental in averting even greater social and economic hardships. However, labour market conditions have continued to deteriorate in many countries and will likely threaten much of the progress made over the last decade towards decent work.

The economic deterioration resulted in a sharp drop in employment-to-population ratios. In addition, labour productivity declined in 2009. In most regions, the decrease in gross domestic product was even greater than the decline in employment, resulting in diminishing output per worker. Preliminary estimates indicate a negative growth in output per worker in all regions except Northern Africa, Eastern Asia and Southern Asia. The largest fall in output per worker was in CIS countries in Europe, the transition countries of South-Eastern Europe and in Latin America and the Caribbean. Declining labour output contributes to poorer working conditions, worsening the plight of workers in regions where labour productivity was already low before the economic crisis, as in sub-Saharan Africa.

As jobs were lost, more workers have been forced into vulnerable employment

Proportion of own-account and contributing family workers in total employment, 1998, 2008 and 2009 second scenario (Percentage)

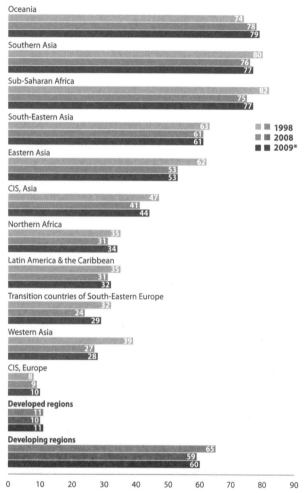

*Forecasts for 2009 are based on the International Labour Organization's second scenario. Details are available at mdgs.un.org

The positive downward trend in vulnerable employment was interrupted by deteriorating conditions on the labour market following the financial crisis. For many wage and salaried workers who lost their jobs, as well as first-time job seekers who entered the labour market in the midst of the crisis, own-account and unpaid family work are options of last resort.

Those engaged in 'vulnerable employment', defined as the sum of own-account workers and contributing family workers, are not typically bound by formal work arrangements. They are therefore more likely to lack benefits associated with decent employment, such as adequate social security and recourse to effective mechanisms for social dialogue. Vulnerable employment is often characterized by inadequate earnings, low productivity and substandard working conditions that undermine fundamental labour rights.

Prior to the economic crisis, over three quarters of workers in Oceania, Southern Asia and sub-Saharan Africa were without the security that wage and salaried jobs could provide. The crisis is likely to have further increased the number of workers engaged in vulnerable employment in these regions in 2009. The International Labour Organization (ILO) estimates* the global vulnerable employment rate in 2009 to be between 49 per cent and 53 per cent, which translates into 1.5 billion to 1.6 billion people who are working on their own or as unpaid family workers worldwide.

* Details are available at http://mdgs.un.org

Since the economic crisis, more workers find themselves and their families living in extreme poverty

Proportion of employed people living below $1.25 a day, 1998, 2008 and 2009 second scenario (Percentage)

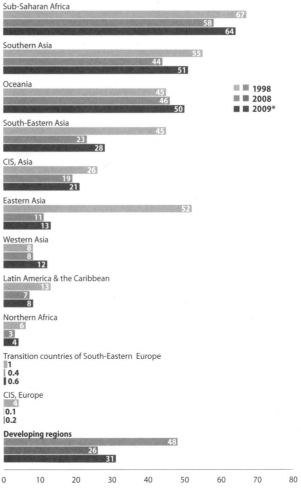

*Data for 2009 are based on the ILO's second scenario.
Details are available at mdgs.un.org

The 'working poor' are defined as those who are employed but live in households where individual members subsist on less than $1.25 a day. Most of these workers are engaged in jobs that lack the social protection and safety nets that guard against times of low economic demand, and they are often unable to generate sufficient savings to offset hard times. Since vulnerable employment is often characterized by low productivity work, and the global financial crisis has resulted in declining output per worker, working poverty is likely to have increased as well. The small decreases in the percentage of working poor in 2009 that would result from a continuation of historical trends (scenario 1) are therefore not likely to have materialized. Rather, it is estimated that an additional 3.6 per cent of the world's workers were at risk of falling into poverty between 2008 and 2009 (scenario 2), an alarming increase and a setback of many years of steady progress.

The largest negative impact is most likely to be seen in sub-Saharan Africa, Southern Asia, South-Eastern Asia and Oceania, where extreme poverty among the employed may have increased by four percentage points or more in the second scenario. These estimates reflect the fact that, prior to the crisis, many workers in these regions were only slightly above the poverty line. In the case of sub-Saharan Africa, the large majority of workers (63.5 per cent) were at risk of falling below the extreme poverty line in this scenario.

TARGET
Halve, between 1990 and 2015, the proportion of people who suffer from hunger

Hunger may have spiked in 2009, one of the many dire consequences of the global food and financial crises

Proportion of people who are undernourished in the developing regions (Percentage) and number of undernourished people (Millions), 1990-1992, 1995-1997, 2000-2002 and 2005-2007

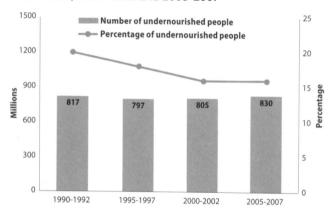

Since 1990, developing regions have made some progress towards the MDG target of halving the proportion of people suffering from hunger. The share of undernourished populations decreased from 20 per cent in 1990-1992 to 16 per cent in 2005-2007, the latest period with available data. However, progress has stalled since 2000-2002. Overall progress in reducing the prevalence of hunger has not been sufficient to reduce the number of undernourished people. In 2005-2007, the last period assessed, 830 million people were still undernourished, an increase from 817 million in 1990-1992.

Food prices spiked in 2008 and falling income due to the financial crisis further worsened the situation. The Food and Agricultural Organization of the United Nations estimates that the number of people who were undernourished in 2008 may be as high as 915 million and exceed 1 billion in 2009.

Progress to end hunger has been stymied in most regions

Prices of staple foods remained high in 2009, after the initial food crisis of 2008. At the same time, the incomes of poor households diminished because of higher unemployment following the economic downturn. Both crises contributed to a considerable reduction in the effective purchasing power of poor consumers, who spend a substantial share of their income on basic foodstuffs.

Though international food prices continued to decline in the second half of 2008, consumer food price indexes rose. International food prices have not yet stabilized and threats of new food crises loom.

Aggregate food availability globally was relatively good in 2008 and 2009, but higher food prices and reduced employment and incomes meant that the poor had less access to that food.

Proportion of undernourished population, 1990-1992, 2000-2002 and 2005-2007 (Percentage)

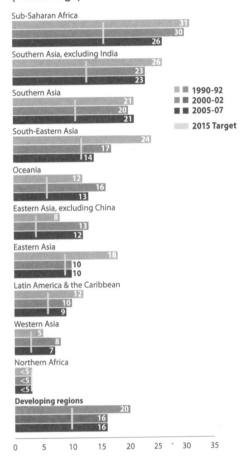

Sub-Saharan Africa
31
30
26

Southern Asia, excluding India
26
23
23

Southern Asia
21
20
21

■ ■ 1990-92
■ ■ 2000-02
■ ■ 2005-07
2015 Target

South-Eastern Asia
24
17
14

Oceania
12
16
13

Eastern Asia, excluding China
8
13
12

Eastern Asia
18
10
10

Latin America & the Caribbean
12
10
9

Western Asia
5
8
7

Northern Africa
<5
<5
<5

Developing regions
20
16
16

0   5   10   15   20   25   30   35

Before the onset of the food and financial crises, a number of regions were well on their way to halving, by 2015, the proportion of their population that were undernourished. South-Eastern Asia, which was already close to the target in 2005-2007 made additional progress, as did Latin America and the Caribbean and Eastern Asia. Progress in the latter region was largely due to reductions in hunger in China. The prevalence of hunger also declined in sub-Saharan Africa, although not at a pace that was sufficiently fast to compensate for population growth and to put the region on track to meet the MDG target.

Despite some progress, one in four children in the developing world are still underweight

Halving the prevalence of underweight children by 2015 (from a 1990 baseline) will require accelerated and concerted action to scale up interventions that effectively combat undernutrition. A number of simple and cost-effective interventions at key stages in a child's life could go a long way in reducing undernutrition, such as breastfeeding within one hour of birth, exclusive breastfeeding for the first six months of life, adequate complementary feeding and micronutrient supplementation between six and 24 months of age.

Undernutrition among children under five continues to be widely prevalent, due to both a lack of food and lack of quality food, inadequate water, sanitation and health services as well as less than optimal caring and feeding practices. Until improvements are made in all these areas, progress will be limited. In Southern Asia, for example, feeding practices are often poor and shortages of quality food are common. But in addition, nearly two thirds of the population are without improved sanitation and nearly half practise open defecation, resulting in repeated episodes of diarrheal diseases in children. Moreover, more than 25 per cent of infants are underweight at birth. Many of these children are never able to catch up in terms of their nutritional status. All of these factors have made underweight prevalence in Southern Asia—at 46 per cent—the highest in the world.

Proportion of children under age five who are underweight, 1990 and 2008 (Percentage)

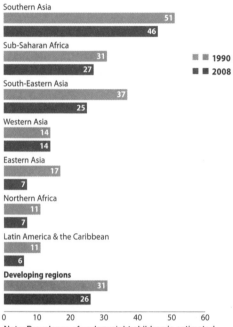

Note: Prevalence of underweight children is estimated based on the NCHS/WHO/CDC reference population. The United Nations Children's Fund (UNICEF) is in the process of converting its entire child undernutrition database according to the new World Health Organization (WHO) Child Growth Standards.

From 1990 to 2008, the proportion of children under five in the developing regions who are underweight declined from 31 per cent to 26 per cent. Progress in reducing underweight prevalence among children has been made in all regions except Western Asia. Eastern Asia, Latin America and the Caribbean, and CIS countries in Asia have reached or nearly reached the MDG target, and South-Eastern Asia and Northern Africa are on track.

Progress is being made, but not fast enough to reach the MDG target. Data are not yet available to fully understand the impact of the food and financial crises on underweight prevalence, but the achievement of the MDG target may be further threatened by them.

Children in rural areas are nearly twice as likely to be underweight as those in urban areas

In some regions, the prevalence of underweight children is dramatically higher among the poor

Ratio between the proportion of under-five children who are underweight in rural areas and urban areas, 1990 and 2008

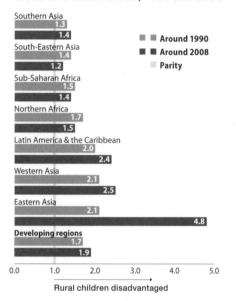

Proportion of under-five children who are underweight, by household wealth, around 2008 (Percentage)

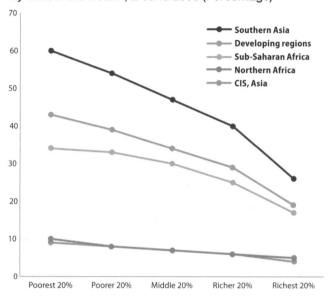

In all developing regions, children in rural areas are more likely to be underweight than children living in cities and towns. In parts of Asia and in Latin America and the Caribbean, the relative disparity actually increased between 1990 and 2008. In Eastern Asia, there was a striking increase in the rural/urban ratio (from 2.1 to 4.8), indicating that, in 2008, children in rural areas were almost five times as likely to be underweight as children in urban areas. This region, however, has already achieved the target—in both rural and urban areas—of halving the 1990 underweight prevalence: only 2 per cent of children in urban areas are underweight, versus 9 per cent of rural children.

South-Eastern Asia, sub-Saharan Africa and Northern Africa have succeeded in reducing child malnutrition more rapidly in rural areas and in narrowing the gap with the urban population, demonstrating that more equitable progress is indeed possible.

Across the developing world, children from the poorest households are twice as likely to be underweight as children from the richest households. The disparity is most dramatic in regions with a high prevalence of underweight children. This is the situation in Southern Asia, where as many as 60 per cent of children in the poorest families are underweight, compared to about 25 per cent in the richest households.

Over 42 million people have been uprooted by conflict or persecution

Number of refugees and internally displaced persons, 2000-2009 (Millions)

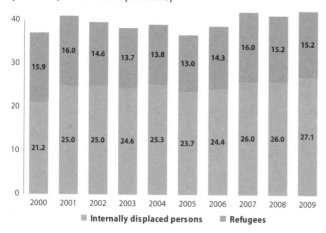

■ **Internally displaced persons**   ■ **Refugees**

Conflicts are a major threat to human security and to hard-won MDG gains. Years after a conflict has ended, large populations of refugees remain in camps with limited employment and education opportunities and inadequate health services. Not surprisingly, refugees often become dependent on subsistence-level assistance and lead lives of poverty and unrealized potential.

More than 42 million people are currently displaced by conflict or persecution. Of these, 15.2 million are refugees (residing outside their countries of origin) and 27.1 million people have been uprooted but remain within the borders of their own countries. Developing countries hosted four fifths of the global refugee population in 2009. They included 10.4 million people who fall under the aegis of the United Nations High Commissioner for Refugees (UNHCR) and 4.8 million Palestinian refugees, who are the responsibility of the United Nations Relief and Works Agency for Palestine Refugees in the Near East (UNRWA).

The number of refugees has remained relatively stable over the past two years—about 15 million—in part because of the lack of durable solutions. In 2009, some 250,000 refugees were able to return to their homes voluntarily, the lowest level in 20 years. Afghans and Iraqis continue to be the largest refugee populations under the UNHCR mandate, totalling 2.9 million and 1.8 million people, respectively, at the end of 2009. Together they account for nearly half of all refugees under UNHCR care.

Goal 2

Achieve universal primary education

TARGET
Ensure that, by 2015, children everywhere, boys and girls alike, will be able to complete a full course of primary schooling

Hope dims for universal education by 2015, even as many poor countries make tremendous strides

Adjusted net enrolment ratio in primary education,* 1998/1999 and 2007/2008 (Percentage)

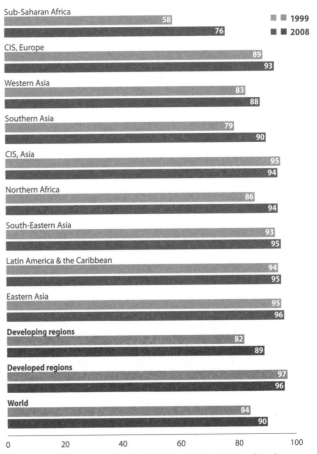

Sub-Saharan Africa — 58 (1999), 76 (2008)
CIS, Europe — 89 (1999), 93 (2008)
Western Asia — 83 (1999), 88 (2008)
Southern Asia — 79 (1999), 90 (2008)
CIS, Asia — 95 (1999), 94 (2008)
Northern Africa — 86 (1999), 94 (2008)
South-Eastern Asia — 93 (1999), 95 (2008)
Latin America & the Caribbean — 94 (1999), 95 (2008)
Eastern Asia — 95 (1999), 96 (2008)
Developing regions — 82 (1999), 89 (2008)
Developed regions — 97 (1999), 96 (2008)
World — 84 (1999), 90 (2008)

■ ■ 1999
■ ■ 2008

0   20   40   60   80   100

* Defined as the number of pupils of the theoretical school age for primary education enrolled in either primary or secondary school, expressed as a percentage of the total population in that age group.

Note: Data for Oceania are not available.

Enrolment in primary education has continued to rise, reaching 89 per cent in the developing world. But the pace of progress is insufficient to ensure that, by 2015, all girls and boys complete a full course of primary schooling.

To achieve the goal by the target date, all children at the official entry age for primary school would have had to be attending classes by 2009 or so, depending on the duration of the primary level and how well schools retain pupils to the end of the cycle. But in half of the sub-Saharan African countries with available data, at least one in four children of primary-school age were out of school in 2008.

To meet the goal, countries will also need to ensure that there are enough teachers and classrooms to meet the demand. Between now and 2015, the number of new teachers needed in sub-Saharan Africa alone equals the current teaching force in the region.

Despite these challenges, a good deal has been accomplished in many regions. Though enrolment in sub-Saharan Africa remains the lowest of all regions, it still increased by 18 percentage points—from 58 per cent to 76 per cent—between 1999 and 2008. Progress was also made in Southern Asia and Northern Africa, where enrolment increased by 11 and 8 percentage points, respectively, over the last decade.

Major advances have been made even in some of the poorest countries, most of them in sub-Saharan Africa. The abolition of primary school fees in Burundi resulted in a threefold increase in primary-school enrolment since 1999, reaching 99 per cent in 2008. Similarly, the United Republic of Tanzania doubled its enrolment ratio over the same period. Guatemala, Nicaragua and Zambia also broke through the 90 per cent threshold towards greater access to primary education.

Getting children into school is a vital first step. But to receive the full benefits of education, they must continue to attend classes. In half the countries in sub-Saharan Africa with available data, more than 30 per cent of primary-school students drop out before reaching the final grade.

Sub-Saharan Africa and Southern Asia are home to the vast majority of children out of school

Distribution of out-of-school children by region, 1999 and 2008 (Percentage)

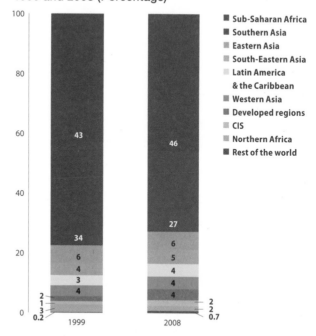

Even as the number of school-age children continues to rise, the total number of children out of school is decreasing—from 106 million in 1999 to 69 million in 2008. Almost half of these children (31 million) are in sub-Saharan Africa, and more than a quarter (18 million) are in Southern Asia.

The gender gap in the out-of-school population has also narrowed: the share of girls in this group decreased from 57 per cent to 53 per cent globally between 1999 and 2008. In some regions, however, the share is much larger; in Northern Africa, 66 per cent of out-of-school children are girls.

Inequality thwarts progress towards universal education

Out-of-school children by wealth quintile and area of residence, girls and boys, 42 countries, 2000/2008 (Percentage)

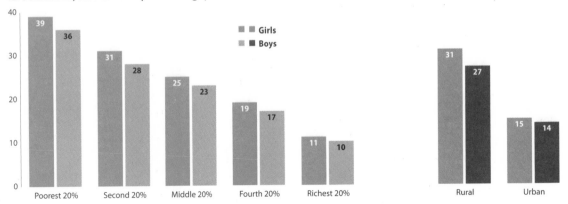

Household data from 42 countries show that rural children are twice as likely to be out of school as children living in urban areas. The data also show that the rural-urban gap is slightly wider for girls than for boys. But the biggest obstacle to education is poverty. Girls in the poorest 20 per cent of households have the least chance of getting an education: they are 3.5 times more likely to be out of school than girls in the richest households and four times more likely to be out of school as boys in the richest households. Boys from the richest households are the least likely to be out of school (10 per cent), compared to all other groups.

Children remain out of school for a variety of reasons, including cost. Social and cultural barriers to education are also common. In many countries, educating girls is widely perceived as being of less value than educating boys. And children with disabilities across the world face far more limited opportunities than their non-disabled peers.

The link between disability and marginalization in education is evident in countries at all levels of development. In Malawi and the United Republic of Tanzania, being disabled doubles the probability that a child will never attend school, and in Burkina Faso the risk rises to two and a half times. Even in some countries that are closer to achieving the goal of universal primary education, children with disabilities represent the majority of those who are excluded. In Bulgaria and Romania, net enrolment ratios for children aged 7 to 15 were over 90 per cent in 2002, but only 58 per cent for children with disabilities.

Goal 3

Promote gender equality and empower women

For girls in some regions, education remains elusive

Girls' primary-school enrolment in relation to boys', 1998/1999 and 2007/2008 (Girls per 100 boys)

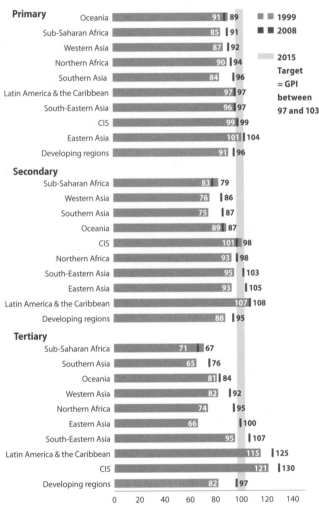

The developing regions as a whole are approaching gender parity in educational enrolment. In 2008, there were 96 girls for every 100 boys enrolled in primary school, and 95 girls for every 100 boys enrolled in secondary school. In 1999, the ratios were 91:100 and 88:100 for the two levels of education, respectively. Despite this progress, gender parity in primary and secondary education—a target that was to be met by

2005—is still out of reach for many developing regions. For primary education, the steepest challenges are found in Oceania, sub-Saharan Africa and Western Asia.

In secondary education, the gender gap in enrolment is most evident in the three regions where overall enrolment is lowest—sub-Saharan Africa, Western Asia and Southern Asia. In contrast, more girls than boys have signed up for secondary school in Latin America and the Caribbean, Eastern Asia and South-Eastern Asia.

In tertiary education, the ratio between girls and boys in the developing regions is close to parity, at 97 girls per 100 boys. This is largely due to the fact that many more girls than boys are enrolled in higher education in the CIS countries, Latin America and the Caribbean, Northern Africa and South-Eastern Asia. But in most other regions, the number of boys heavily outweighs that of girls in colleges and universities. In sub-Saharan Africa and Southern Asia, for example, only 67 and 76 girls per 100 boys, respectively, are enrolled in tertiary levels of education.

Other gender disparities found in tertiary education relate to areas of study, with women being overrepresented in the humanities and social sciences and significantly underrepresented in science, technology and, in particular, engineering. Completion rates also tend to be lower among women than men.

Poverty is a major barrier to education, especially among older girls

Proportion of girls and boys who are out of school, by age and household wealth, in 42 countries with surveys during 2001/2008 (Percentage)

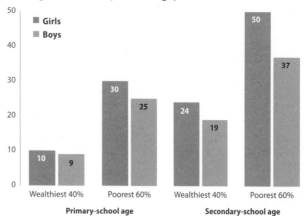

Poverty puts girls at a distinct disadvantage in terms of education. Girls of primary-school age from the poorest 60 per cent of households are three times more likely to be out of school as those from the wealthiest households. Their chances of attending secondary school are even slimmer, and older girls in general are more likely to be out of school. In the poorest households, about twice as many girls of secondary-school age are out of school compared to their wealthier peers.

Household survey data also indicate that girls in rural areas face added challenges in getting an education and that the gender gap is much wider for girls of secondary-school age.

In every developing region except the CIS, men outnumber women in paid employment

Employees in non-agricultural wage employment who are women, 1990–2008, and projections to 2015 (Percentage)

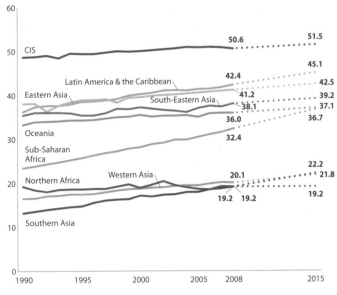

Globally, the share of women in paid employment outside the agricultural sector has continued to increase slowly and reached 41 per cent in 2008. But women in some regions are seriously lagging behind. In Southern Asia, Northern Africa and Western Asia, only 20 per cent of those employed outside agriculture are women. Gender equality in the labour market is also a concern in sub-Saharan Africa, where only one in three paid jobs outside of agriculture are occupied by women.

But even when women represent a large share of waged workers, it does not mean that they have secure, decent jobs. In fact, women are typically paid less and have less secure employment than men.

In countries where the agricultural sector predominates, women are mostly employed in agriculture and largely in vulnerable jobs—in subsistence farming, as unpaid family workers or as own-account workers—with no or little financial security or social benefits.

Women are largely relegated to more vulnerable forms of employment

Proportion of own-account and contributing family workers in total employment, 2009 projections (Percentage)

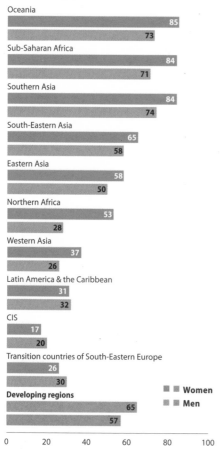

The 2008 financial crisis has eroded employment around the world. As both women and men lost their jobs, unemployment rates shot up, especially in the first half of 2009. The good news is that the rate at which unemployment is increasing appears to be slowing, according to the latest data. However, the fact that women are disproportionately represented in temporary employment, and occupy a substantial share of jobs in export-oriented manufacturing industries in many developing countries, may result in higher unemployment rates for women.

While the crisis has drawn attention to the levels of unemployment, the *quality* of available jobs is also worrisome. Many wage and salaried workers who lost their jobs, as well as many first-time job seekers who entered the labour market in the midst of the financial turmoil, have resorted to own-account or unpaid family work, resulting in deteriorating working conditions and lower incomes for the poorest. Women are more likely than men to be in vulnerable jobs, with the gap being particularly evident in those regions where paid employment opportunities for women are the lowest—in Western Asia and Northern Africa.

Women are overrepresented in informal employment, with its lack of benefits and security

Top-level jobs still go to men — to an overwhelming degree

Informal employment as a percentage of total non-agricultural employment, women and men, selected countries, 2003/2005 (Percentage)

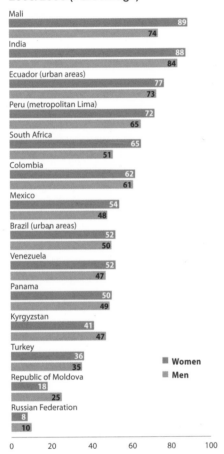

Share of women in top-level and all occupations, average for the period 2000/2008 (Percentage)

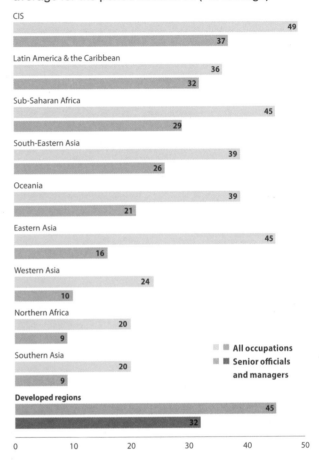

It is likely that the recent financial crisis has also led to a surge in informal employment due to job losses in the formal sector. In some developing countries, over 80 per cent of workers have informal jobs—as owners of informal-sector businesses, contributing family workers or employees without written contracts or social security benefits (including subcontracted workers operating from home and domestic services workers). In most of these countries, women are overrepresented in informal employment.

Though the number of women who secured paid jobs outside the agricultural sector increased between 1990 and 2008, women have generally failed to access higher-level positions. The top jobs—as senior officials or managers—are still dominated by men. Globally, only one in four senior officials or managers are women. And in all regions, women are underrepresented among high-level workers, accounting for 30 per cent or more of such positions in only three out of 10 regions. In Western Asia, Southern Asia and Northern Africa, less than 10 per cent of top-level positions are held by women.

Women are slowly rising to political power, but mainly when boosted by quotas and other special measures

Proportion of seats held by women in single or lower houses of national parliaments, 2000 and 2010 (Percentage)

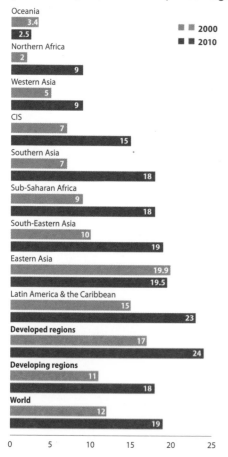

officers in 269 parliamentary chambers (13 per cent) in January 2010, up from 24 in 1995.

Following parliamentary elections and renewals in 2009, gains for women were registered in sub-Saharan Africa, where 29 per cent of the renewed seats went to women, bringing the regional average up to 18 per cent. In South Africa, women took 44 per cent of seats in the lower-house election, placing it third in terms of global ranking, after Rwanda and Sweden. Similarly, there was some progress in most countries in Latin America and the Caribbean, with 25 per cent of seats up for renewal going to women. Bolivia's upper house elected more than 40 per cent women members, bringing the regional average up to 23 per cent.

At the opposite end of the spectrum, 58 countries have 10 per cent or fewer women members of parliament and, in nine chambers, women have no seats at all. During 2009, no women gained seats in parliamentary renewals in the Comoros, the Federated States of Micronesia and Saudi Arabia.

Electoral systems, quota arrangements and other affirmative action measures taken by political parties continue to be key predictors of progress for women. During 2009, the average share of women elected to parliament reached 27 per cent in countries that applied such measures; in contrast, women gained only a 14 per cent share of seats in countries that did not. Women are also elected in far greater numbers under systems of proportional representation, rather than majority/plurality systems.

In addition to electoral systems and quotas, gender-sensitive electoral arrangements, well-trained and financed women candidates and political will at the highest levels of political parties and governments are key to overcoming gender imbalances in the world's parliaments. Given that there are still four men for every one woman in parliament, efforts will be needed on all these fronts if the target of 30 per cent is to be met.

The global share of women in parliament continues to increase slowly and reached an all-time high of 19 per cent in 2010. This represents a gain of 67 per cent since 1995, when 11 per cent of parliamentarians worldwide were women. But it is far short of the target of 30 per cent of women in leadership positions that was to be met by 1995, and further still from the MDG target of gender parity.

Women make up 30 per cent or more of the members of lower houses of parliament in 26 countries and 40 per cent or more in seven countries. There were 35 women presiding

Progress in achieving greater representation by women in the executive branches of government is even slower than in the legislative branches. In 2010, just nine of 151 elected heads of state (6 per cent) and 11 of 192 heads of government (6 per cent) were women. This is an improvement over 2008, when only seven women were elected as heads of state and eight as heads of government. On average, women hold 16 per cent of ministerial posts and only 30 countries have more than 30 per cent women ministers. On the other hand, 16 countries have no women ministers at all. The majority of these countries are in Northern Africa and Western Asia, the Caribbean and Oceania.

Goal 4

Reduce child mortality

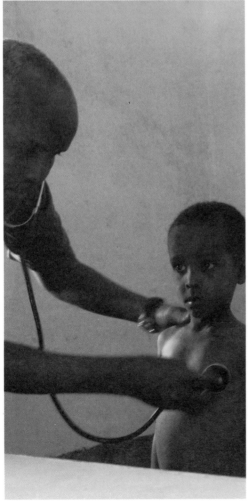

Child deaths are falling, but not quickly enough to reach the target

Under-five mortality rate per 1,000 live births, 1990 and 2008

Region	1990	2008
Sub-Saharan Africa	184	144
Southern Asia	121	74
Oceania	76	60
CIS, Asia	78	39
South-Eastern Asia	73	38
Western Asia	66	32
Northern Africa	80	29
Latin America & the Caribbean	52	23
Eastern Asia	45	21
CIS, Europe	26	14
Transition countries of South-Eastern Europe	30	12
Developed regions	12	6
Developing regions	100	72

■ ■ 1990
■ ■ 2008
2015 Target

0   50   100   150   200

Substantial progress has been made in reducing child deaths. Since 1990, the mortality rate for children under age five in developing countries dropped by 28 per cent—from 100 deaths per 1,000 live births to 72 in 2008. Globally, the total number of under-five deaths declined from 12.5 million in 1990 to 8.8 million in 2008. This means that, in 2008, 10,000 fewer children died each day than in 1990. An encouraging sign is the acceleration of progress after the year 2000: the average annual rate of decline increased to 2.3 per cent for the period 2000 to 2008, compared to 1.4 per cent in the 1990s.

The greatest advances were made in Northern Africa, Eastern Asia, Western Asia, Latin America and the Caribbean, and the countries of the CIS. But most striking is the progress that has been made in some of the world's poorest countries. Against steep odds, Bangladesh, Bolivia, Eritrea, Lao People's Democratic Republic, Malawi, Mongolia and Nepal have all reduced their under-five mortality rates by 4.5 per cent annually or more. Ethiopia, Malawi, Mozambique and Niger have seen absolute reductions of more than 100 per 1,000 live births since 1990.

Despite these achievements, and the fact that most child deaths are preventable or treatable, many countries still have unacceptably high levels of child mortality and have made little or no progress in recent years. What's more, among the 67 countries with high child mortality rates (defined as 40 or more deaths per 1,000 live births), only 10 are on track to meet the MDG target on child survival. The highest rates of child mortality continue to be found in sub-Saharan Africa. In 2008, one in seven children there died before their fifth birthday; the highest levels were in Western and Central Africa, where one in six children died before age five (169 deaths per 1,000 live births). All 34 countries with under-five mortality rates exceeding 100 per 1,000 live births in 2008 are in sub-Saharan Africa, except Afghanistan. Although under-five mortality in sub-Saharan Africa has declined by 22 per cent since 1990, the rate of improvement is insufficient to meet the target. Furthermore, high levels of fertility, combined with a still large percentage of under-five deaths, have resulted in an increase in the absolute number of children who have died—from 4.0 million in 1990 to 4.4 million in 2008. Sub-Saharan Africa accounted for half of the 8.8 million deaths in children under five worldwide in 2008.

Under-five mortality also remains very high in Southern Asia, where about one in 14 children died before age five in 2008 and where progress is too slow to meet the 2015 target.

Revitalizing efforts against pneumonia and diarrhoea, while bolstering nutrition, could save millions of children

Causes of deaths among children under age five, 2008 (Percentage)

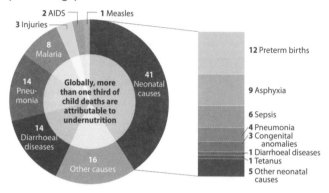

Four diseases—pneumonia, diarrhoea, malaria and AIDS—accounted for 43 per cent of all deaths in children under five worldwide in 2008. Most of these lives could have been saved through low-cost prevention and treatment measures, including antibiotics for acute respiratory infections, oral rehydration for diarrhoea, immunization, and the use of insecticide-treated mosquito nets and appropriate drugs for malaria. The need to refocus attention on pneumonia and diarrhoea—two of the three leading killers of children—is urgent. The use of new tools, such as vaccines against pneumococcal pneumonia and rotaviral diarrhoea, could add momentum to the fight against these common diseases and provide an entry point for the revitalization of comprehensive programming. Ensuring proper nutrition is a critical aspect of prevention, since malnutrition increases the risk of death.

Recent success in controlling measles may be short-lived if funding gaps are not bridged

Proportion of children 12-23 months old who received at least one dose of measles vaccine, 2000 and 2008 (Percentage)

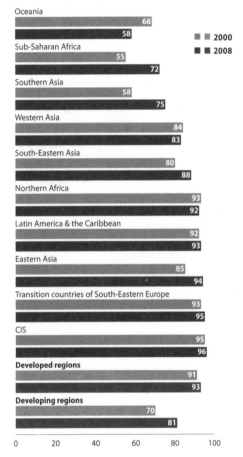

Oceania: 68 (2000), 58 (2008)
Sub-Saharan Africa: 55 (2000), 72 (2008)
Southern Asia: 58 (2000), 75 (2008)
Western Asia: 84 (2000), 83 (2008)
South-Eastern Asia: 80 (2000), 88 (2008)
Northern Africa: 93 (2000), 92 (2008)
Latin America & the Caribbean: 92 (2000), 93 (2008)
Eastern Asia: 85 (2000), 94 (2008)
Transition countries of South-Eastern Europe: 93 (2000), 95 (2008)
CIS: 95 (2000), 96 (2008)
Developed regions: 91 (2000), 93 (2008)
Developing regions: 70 (2000), 81 (2008)

Legend: 2000, 2008

Globally, routine immunization against measles has continued to rise and protect millions of children against this often fatal disease. In 2008, coverage reached 81 per cent in the developing regions as a whole, up from 70 per cent in 2000. Such averages, however, mask significant inequalities in access to the vaccine. Data from 178 Demographic and Health Surveys suggest that access to measles vaccinations varies across different social and economic groups, with lower coverage for children in households that are poor or located in rural areas, or whose parents have lower levels of education. Higher birth order (that is, having many older siblings) is also associated with lower measles vaccine coverage. Disparities between girls and boys in immunization coverage are not significant, except in some South Asian countries.

A single-dose vaccine strategy is not sufficient to prevent measles outbreaks. As of 2008, a total of 132 countries used a two-dose schedule routinely. In countries with weak health systems, the second dose is offered during campaigns to ensure high coverage. Between 2000 and 2008, the combination of improved routine immunization coverage and the provision of a second-dose opportunity led to a 78 per cent reduction in measles deaths globally—from an estimated 733,000 deaths in 2000 to 164,000 in 2008.

But recent successes may be short-lived. Funding for measles-control activities has recently declined, and many priority countries are confronting funding gaps for immunization campaigns. Projections show that without supplementary immunization activities in these countries, mortality will quickly rebound, resulting in approximately 1.7 million measles-related deaths between 2010 and 2013. However, with sufficient funding, political commitment and high-quality implementation of the second-dose measles strategy in priority countries, the exceptional gains made so far can be maintained.

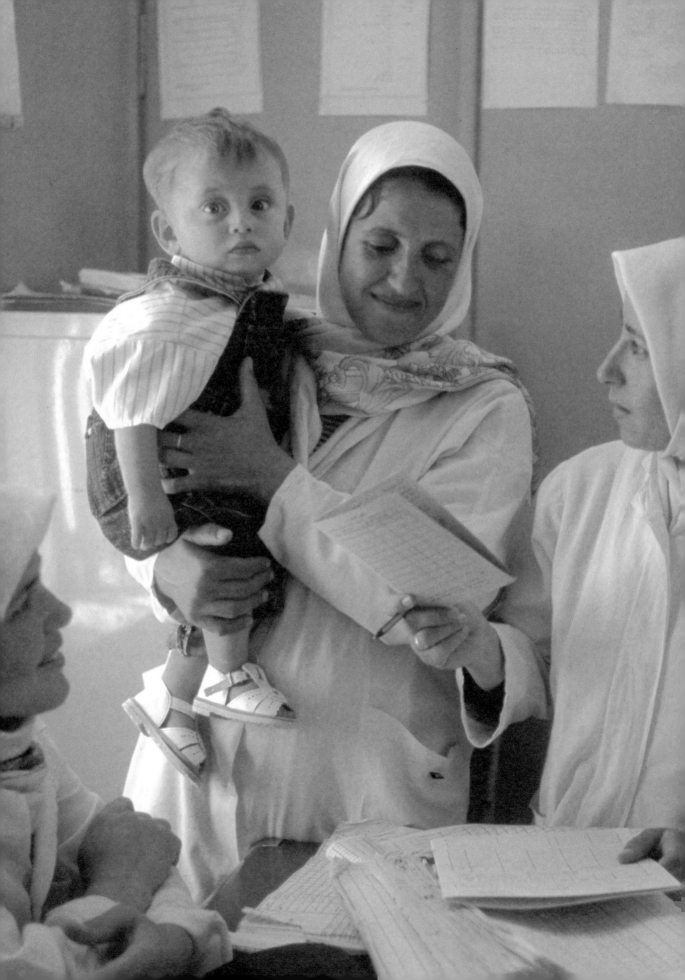

Goal 5

Improve maternal health

TARGET
Reduce by three quarters, between 1990 and 2015, the maternal mortality ratio

Achieving good maternal health requires quality reproductive health services and a series of well-timed interventions to ensure a women's safe passage to motherhood. Failure to provide these results in hundreds of thousands of needless deaths each year—a sad reminder of the low status accorded to women in many societies.

Measuring maternal mortality—death resulting from the complications of pregnancy or childbirth—is challenging at best. Systematic underreporting and misreporting are common, and estimates lie within large ranges of uncertainty. Nevertheless, an acceleration in the provision of maternal and reproductive health services to women in all regions, along with positive trend data on maternal mortality and morbidity, suggest that the world is making some progress on MDG 5.

New estimates of maternal mortality are currently being finalized by the World Health Organization (WHO), the United Nations Children's Fund (UNICEF), the United Nations Population Fund (UNFPA) and the World Bank. Preliminary data show signs of progress, with some countries achieving significant declines in maternal mortality ratios. However, the rate of reduction is still well short of the 5.5 per cent annual decline needed to meet the MDG target. The complete data set will be available at mdgs.un.org

Most maternal deaths could be avoided

Causes of maternal deaths, developing regions, 1997/2007 (Percentage)

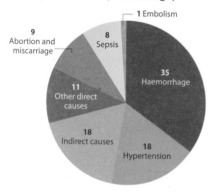

The leading causes of maternal mortality in developing regions are haemorrhage and hypertension, which together account for half of all deaths in expectant or new mothers. Indirect causes, including malaria, HIV/AIDS and heart disease, result in 18 per cent of maternal deaths. Other direct causes, such as obstructed labour, complications of anaesthesia or caesarean section, and ectopic pregnancy, lead to 11 per cent of all deaths during pregnancy or childbirth.

The vast majority of these deaths are avoidable. Haemorrhage, for example, which accounts for over one third of maternal deaths, can be prevented or managed through a range of interventions administered by a skilled health-care provider with adequate equipment and supplies.

Giving birth is especially risky in Southern Asia and sub-Saharan Africa, where most women deliver without skilled care

Proportion of deliveries attended by skilled health personnel, 1990 and 2008 (Percentage)

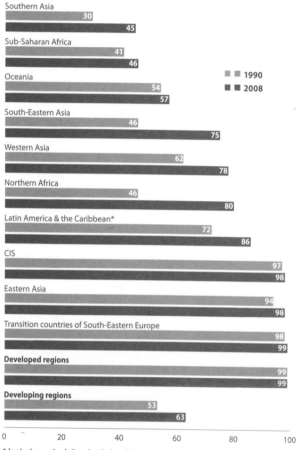

* Includes only deliveries in health-care institutions.

The proportion of women in developing countries who received skilled assistance during delivery rose from 53 per cent in 1990 to 63 per cent in 2008. Progress was made in all regions, but was especially dramatic in Northern Africa and South-Eastern Asia, with increases of 74 per cent and 63 per cent, respectively. Southern Asia also progressed, although coverage there, as well as in sub-Saharan Africa, remains inadequate. Less than half the women giving birth in these regions are attended by skilled health personnel.

The rural-urban gap in skilled care during childbirth has narrowed

Ratio of urban women to rural women attended by skilled health personnel during delivery, 1990 and 2008

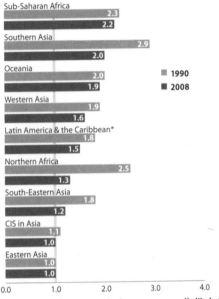

■ Parity: Rural women and urban women equally likely to receive skilled care at delivery

* Includes only deliveries in health-care institutions.

More rural women are receiving skilled assistance during delivery, reducing long-standing disparities between urban and rural areas. In Southern Asia, for example, urban women were three times more likely as their rural counterparts to receive professional care at childbirth in 1990; by 2008, they were only twice as likely to receive such care, indicating some improvement. Still, inequalities persist, especially in regions where attendance by skilled personnel is lowest and maternal mortality highest—notably in sub-Saharan Africa, Southern Asia and Oceania.

Serious disparities in coverage are also found between the wealthiest and the poorest households. The widest gaps are in Southern Asia and sub-Saharan Africa, where the wealthiest women are five times more likely and three times more likely, respectively, as the poorest women to be attended by trained health-care workers at delivery. In the developing regions as a whole, women in the richest households are three times as likely as women in the poorest households to receive professional care during childbirth.

More women are receiving antenatal care

Proportion of women attended at least once during pregnancy by skilled health-care personnel, 1990 and 2008 (Percentage)

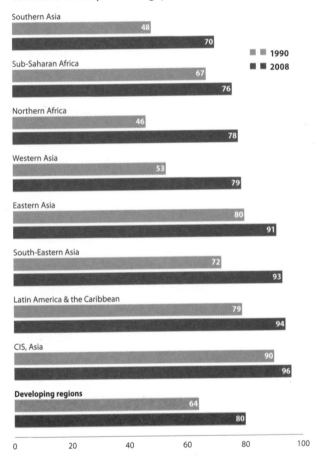

In all regions, progress is being made in providing pregnant women with antenatal care. Remarkable gains were recorded in Northern Africa, where the share of women who saw a skilled health worker at least once during pregnancy increased by 70 per cent. Southern Asia and Western Asia reported increases of almost 50 per cent.

Inequalities in care during pregnancy are striking

Proportion of women attended at least once during pregnancy by skilled health personnel, by household wealth quintile, 2003/2008 (Percentage)

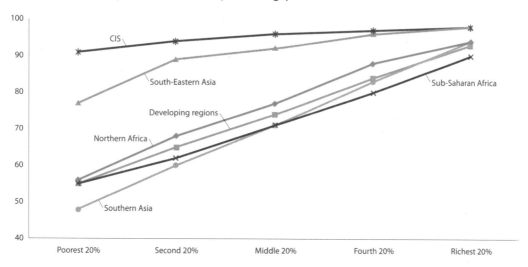

Disparities in the share of women receiving antenatal care by wealth are striking, particularly in Southern Asia, Northern Africa and sub-Saharan Africa. Even in South-Eastern Asia, where over 90 per cent of women receive skilled care during pregnancy, only 77 per cent of women in the poorest households are covered, versus almost 100 per cent of women in the wealthiest households.

Large disparities also exist between women living in rural and urban areas, although the gap narrowed between 1990 and 2008. In sub-Saharan Africa, the proportion of urban women who received antenatal care at least once increased from 84 per cent in 1990 to 89 per cent in 2008. The corresponding proportions for rural women are 55 to 66 per cent, indicating that coverage has improved at a faster pace among rural women.

Only one in three rural women in developing regions receive the recommended care during pregnancy

Progress has stalled in reducing the number of teenage pregnancies, putting more young mothers at risk

Proportion of women attended four or more times during pregnancy by area of residence, 2003/2008 (Percentage)

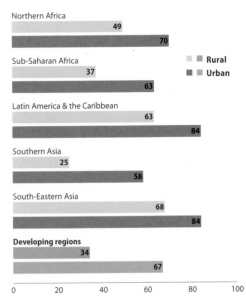

Northern Africa
- Rural: 49
- Urban: 70

Sub-Saharan Africa
- Rural: 37
- Urban: 63

Latin America & the Caribbean
- Rural: 63
- Urban: 84

Southern Asia
- Rural: 25
- Urban: 58

South-Eastern Asia
- Rural: 68
- Urban: 84

Developing regions
- Rural: 34
- Urban: 67

■ Rural
■ Urban

Women should receive care from a trained health-care practitioner at least four times during the course of their pregnancies, according to WHO and UNICEF recommendations. However, less than half of pregnant women in developing regions and only a third of rural women receive the recommended four visits. Among rural women in Southern Asia, the share is only 25 per cent.

Number of births per 1,000 women aged 15-19, 1990, 2000 and 2007

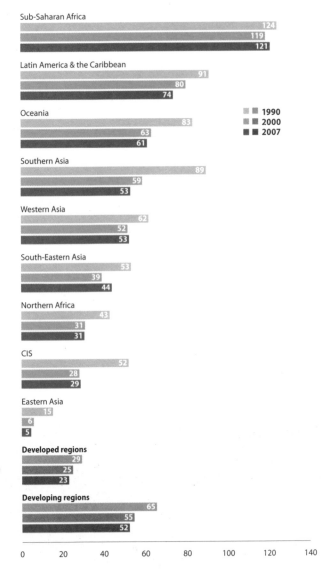

Sub-Saharan Africa
- 1990: 124
- 2000: 119
- 2007: 121

Latin America & the Caribbean
- 1990: 91
- 2000: 80
- 2007: 74

Oceania
- 1990: 83
- 2000: 63
- 2007: 61

Southern Asia
- 1990: 89
- 2000: 59
- 2007: 53

Western Asia
- 1990: 62
- 2000: 52
- 2007: 53

South-Eastern Asia
- 1990: 53
- 2000: 39
- 2007: 44

Northern Africa
- 1990: 43
- 2000: 31
- 2007: 31

CIS
- 1990: 52
- 2000: 28
- 2007: 29

Eastern Asia
- 1990: 15
- 2000: 6
- 2007: 5

Developed regions
- 1990: 29
- 2000: 25
- 2007: 23

Developing regions
- 1990: 65
- 2000: 55
- 2007: 52

■ 1990
■ 2000
■ 2007

In all regions, the adolescent birth rate (the number of births per 1,000 women aged 15 to 19) decreased between 1990 and 2000. Since that time, progress has slowed and, in some regions, increases have even been recorded. The highest birth rate among adolescents is found in sub-Saharan Africa, which has seen little progress since 1990. Adolescents, in general, face greater obstacles than adult women in accessing reproductive health services.

Poverty and lack of education perpetuate high adolescent birth rates

Adolescent birth rates by background characteristics in 24 sub-Saharan African countries, 1998/2008 (Number of births to women aged 15-19 per 1,000 women)

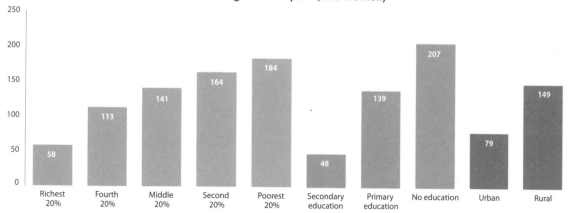

Data for 24 countries in sub-Saharan Africa show that adolescents in the poorest households are three times more likely to become pregnant and give birth than those in the richest households. In rural areas, adolescent birth rates are almost double those of urban areas. But the largest disparities are linked to education: girls with a secondary education are the least likely to become mothers. The birth rate among girls with no education is over four times higher.

Even more worrisome is the widening of disparities over time. The adolescent birth rate declined in 18 of the 24 sub-Saharan countries studied. However, in almost all these 18 countries the decline was largest among adolescents living in urban areas, among those with at least a secondary education, and among those belonging to the richest 20 per cent of households. Thus, disparities between those groups and rural, less educated and poorer adolescents have increased, rather than decreased, over time.

Progress in expanding the use of contraceptives by women has slowed

Proportion of women who are using any method of contraception among women aged 15-49, married or in union, 1990, 2000 and 2007 (Percentage)

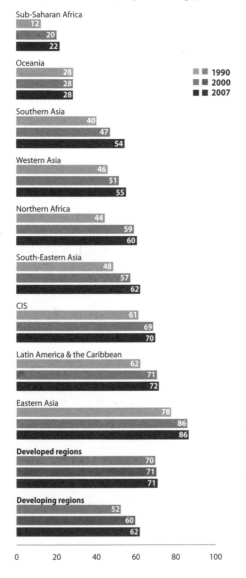

2000 and a widening gap among regions. From 2000 to 2007, the annual rate of increase in contraceptive prevalence in almost all regions was lower than it had been during the 1990s. Moreover, contraceptive prevalence in sub-Saharan Africa and Oceania continues to be very low. And in several subregions, traditional and less effective methods of contraception are still widely used.

Satisfying women's unmet need for family planning—that is, facilitating access to modern contraceptives by women who desire to delay or avoid pregnancy but who are currently not using contraception—could improve maternal health and reduce the number of maternal deaths. Recent estimates indicate that meeting that need could result in a 27 per cent drop in maternal deaths each year by reducing the annual number of unintended pregnancies from 75 million to 22 million. Preventing closely spaced pregnancies and pregnancies among adolescents would also improve the health of women and girls and increase the chances that their children will survive.

The unmet need for family planning remains moderate to high in most regions, particularly in sub-Saharan Africa, where one in four women aged 15 to 49 who are married or in union and have expressed the desire to use contraceptives do not have access to them.

During the 1990s, use of contraceptives increased among women in almost every region. By 2007, over 60 per cent of women aged 15 to 49 who were married or in union were using some form of contraception. Yet this average masks two disturbing trends: a considerable slowdown in progress since

Use of contraception is lowest among the poorest women and those with no education

Contraceptive prevalence by background characteristics in 22 sub-Saharan African countries, surveys around 1994-2003 and 1998-2008 (Percentage of women using at least one contraceptive method among women aged 15-49, married or in union)

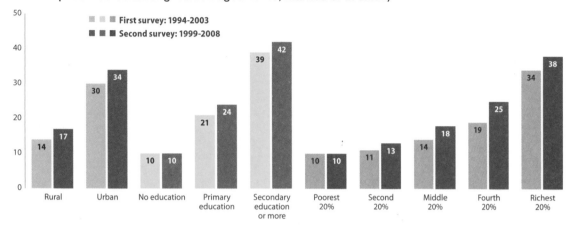

First survey: 1994-2003
Second survey: 1999-2008

	First survey	Second survey
Rural	14	17
Urban	30	34
No education	10	10
Primary education	21	24
Secondary education or more	39	42
Poorest 20%	10	10
Second 20%	11	13
Middle 20%	14	18
Fourth 20%	19	25
Richest 20%	34	38

Ensuring that family planning services reach poor women and those with little education remains particularly challenging. Surveys conducted in 22 countries in sub-Saharan Africa show that contraceptive use to avoid or delay pregnancy is lowest among rural women, among women with no schooling and among those living in the poorest households.

In these countries, contraceptive use is four times higher among women with a secondary education than among those with no education, and is almost four times higher among women in the richest households than those in the poorest households. Almost no improvement has been made over time in increasing contraceptive prevalence among women in the poorest households and among those with no education.

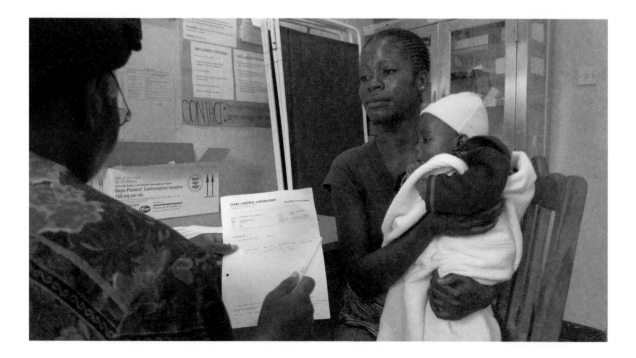

Inadequate funding for family planning is a major failure in fulfilling commitments to improving women's reproductive health

Official development assistance to health, total (Constant 2008 US$ millions) and proportion going to reproductive health care and family planning, 2000-2008 (Percentage)

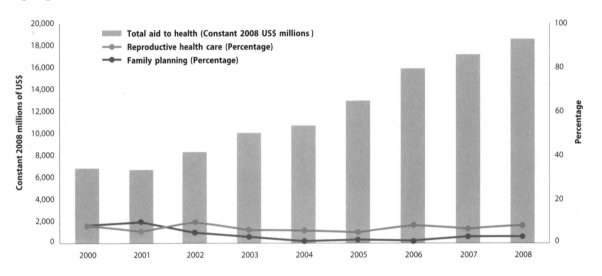

Ensuring that even the poorest and most marginalized women can freely decide the timing and spacing of their pregnancies requires targeted policies and adequately funded interventions. Yet financial resources for family planning services and supplies have not kept pace with demand. Aid for family planning as a proportion of total aid to health declined sharply between 2000 and 2008, from 8.2 per cent to 3.2 per cent. Aid to reproductive health services has fluctuated between 8.1 per cent and 8.5 per cent. External funding for family planning in constant 2008 US dollars actually declined during the first few years of this decade and has not yet returned to its 2000 level.

Goal 6

Combat HIV/AIDS, malaria & other diseases

TARGET
Have halted by 2015 and begun to reverse the spread of HIV/AIDS

The spread of HIV appears to have stabilized in most regions, and more people are surviving longer

Number of people living with HIV, number of people newly infected with HIV and number of AIDS deaths worldwide, 1990-2008 (Millions)

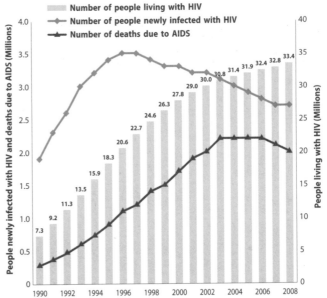

Legend:
- Number of people living with HIV
- Number of people newly infected with HIV
- Number of deaths due to AIDS

People newly infected with HIV and deaths due to AIDS (Millions) — left axis
People living with HIV (Millions) — right axis

People living with HIV values: 7.3, 9.2, 11.3, 13.5, 15.9, 18.3, 20.6, 22.7, 24.6, 26.3, 27.8, 29.0, 30.0, 30.8, 31.4, 31.9, 32.4, 32.8, 33.4

The latest epidemiological data indicate that, globally, the spread of HIV appears to have peaked in 1996, when 3.5 million* people were newly infected. By 2008, that number had dropped to an estimated 2.7 million. AIDS-related mortality peaked in 2004, with 2.2 million deaths. By 2008, that toll had dropped to 2 million, although HIV remains the world's leading infectious killer.

The epidemic appears to have stabilized in most regions, although prevalence continues to rise in Eastern Europe, Central Asia and other parts of Asia due to a high rate of new HIV infections. Sub-Saharan Africa remains the most heavily affected region, accounting for 72 per cent of all new HIV infections in 2008.

* All AIDS-related figures cited are the midpoint in a range. The estimate of 3.5 million new infections, for example, is based on a range of 3.2 million-3.8 million. The complete data series of ranges and corresponding midpoints is available at mdgs.un.org

Though new infections have peaked, the number of people living with the virus is still rising, largely due to the life-sustaining impact of antiretroviral therapy. An estimated 33.4 million people were living with HIV in 2008, of whom 22.4 million are in sub-Saharan Africa.

Many young people still lack the knowledge to protect themselves against HIV

Women and men aged 15–24 with comprehensive correct knowledge of HIV in developing countries, 2003/2008 (Percentage)

Women aged 15–24 (87 countries)

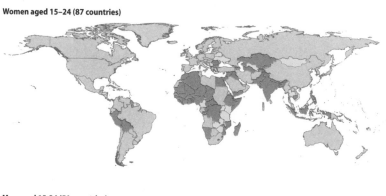

Men aged 15-24 (51 countries)

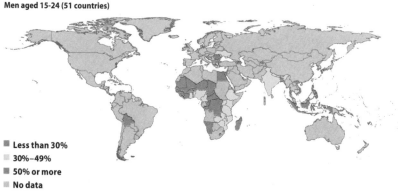

■ Less than 30%
30%–49%
■ 50% or more
No data

Understanding how to prevent transmission of HIV is the first step to avoiding infection. This is especially important for young people (aged 15 to 24), who, in 2008, accounted for 40 per cent of new HIV infections among adults worldwide. Though some progress has been made, comprehensive and correct knowledge of HIV among young people is still unacceptably low in most countries. Less than one third of young men and less than one fifth of young women in developing countries claim such knowledge about HIV. The lowest levels (8 per cent) are found among young women in Northern Africa, according to surveys undertaken between 2003 and 2008. These levels are well below the 2010 target of 95 per cent set at the United Nations General Assembly Special Session on HIV/AIDS in 2001.

Empowering women through AIDS education is indeed possible, as a number of countries have shown

achieved among young men in 8 out of 16 countries. Between 2000 and 2008, Cambodia, Guyana, Namibia, Rwanda, and Trinidad and Tobago reported remarkable increases in knowledge about HIV prevention among young women (reaching levels of 50 per cent or more); similar progress was reported among young men in Namibia and Rwanda.

In sub-Saharan Africa, knowledge of HIV increases with wealth and among those living in urban areas

Young women aged 15-24 with comprehensive correct knowledge of HIV in selected countries, 2000 and 2007 (Percentage)

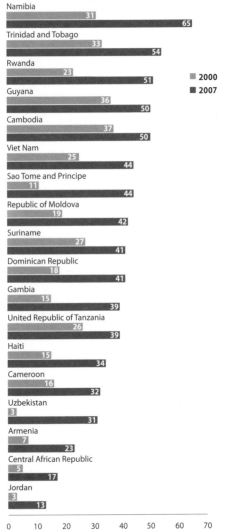

Young women and men aged 15-24 years in selected sub-Saharan African countries with comprehensive correct knowledge of HIV by sex, residence and wealth status, 2003/2008 (Percentage)

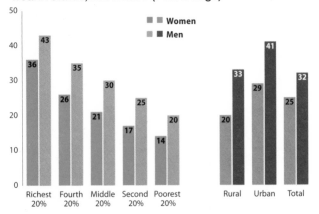

In sub-Saharan Africa, disparities in knowledge about HIV prevention among women and men aged 15 to 24 are linked to gender, household wealth and place of residence. For both men and women, the likelihood of being informed about HIV increases with the income level of one's household. Gender disparities in knowledge also diminish slightly among the rich and among those living in urban areas.

A number of countries have made impressive strides in educating their young people about HIV, despite disappointing global and regional averages. In 18 out of 49 countries with available trend data, comprehensive and correct knowledge of HIV increased by 10 percentage points or more among women aged 15 to 24; the same success was

Disparities are found in condom use by women and men and among those from the richest and poorest households

Condom use during high-risk sex is gaining acceptance in some countries and is one facet of effective HIV prevention

Young women and men aged 15-24 years in selected sub-Saharan African countries who used a condom with the last higher-risk sexual partner by sex, residence and wealth status, 2003/2008 (Percentage)

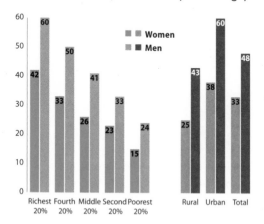

Condom use at last higher-risk sex among young women aged 15-24 in selected countries, 2000 and 2007 (Percentage)

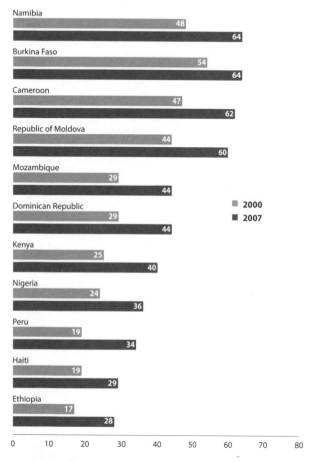

In most developing countries, the majority of young people fail to use condoms during sex, even when there is the risk of contracting HIV. On average, less than 50 per cent of young men and less than a third of young women used condoms during their last higher-risk sexual activity.

In sub-Saharan Africa, men aged 15 to 24 are far more likely to use condoms than women of the same age. For both women and men, condom use increases dramatically with wealth and among those living in urban areas. Similar disparities were observed in all countries with available data.

Although the use of condoms during high-risk sex remains low overall, young people in some countries are proving that the right policies and interventions can yield results. Between 2000 and 2008, increases of 10 or more percentage points in condom use during risky sex were reported among women in 11 of the 22 countries where trends can be documented, reaching levels of 60 per cent or more in some of them. A similar increase was found among men in 11 of 17 countries with available trend data. Such progress is ultimately the result of individual action, supported by a combination of behavioural, biomedical and structural interventions and the collective efforts of government, development partners and civil society.

Mounting evidence shows a link between gender-based violence and HIV

A wide gap exists between knowledge of HIV and preventive action, sometimes due to cultural mores. A tradition of child marriage, for example, can put girls at risk. An analysis of survey data from eight countries shows that young women (aged 15 to 24) who had their sexual debut before age 15 are more likely to be HIV-positive. Tacit social acceptance of violence against women and girls compounds the problem. In four countries surveyed, nearly one in four young women reported that their first experience of sexual intercourse was forced, which increases the chances of contracting HIV.

In fact, growing evidence links gender-based violence with the spread of HIV, underscoring the importance of reaching adolescents through comprehensive prevention programmes that combine a variety of interventions. It also points to the continuing need for social change, so that violence against women and girls in any form is treated with zero tolerance. Enacting and enforcing laws that make such violence punishable as a crime is another part of the solution.

Children orphaned by AIDS suffer more than the loss of parents

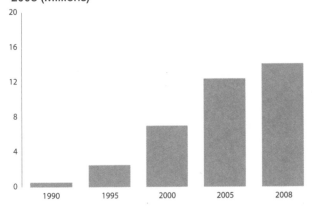

Estimated number of children (0-17 years) who have lost one or both parents due to AIDS in sub-Saharan Africa, 2008 (Millions)

An estimated 17.5 million children (under age 18) lost one or both parents to AIDS in 2008. The vast majority of these children—14.1 million—live in sub-Saharan Africa.

Children orphaned by AIDS are at greater risk of poor health, education and protection than children who have lost parents for other reasons. They are also more likely to be malnourished, sick, or subject to child labour, abuse and neglect, or sexual exploitation—all of which increase their vulnerability to HIV infection. Such children frequently suffer from stigma and discrimination and may be denied access to basic services such as education and shelter as well as opportunities for play.

TARGET
Achieve, by 2010, universal access to treatment for
HIV/AIDS for all those who need it

The rate of new HIV infections continues to outstrip the expansion of treatment

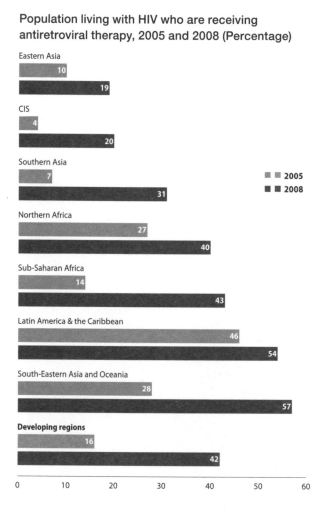

Population living with HIV who are receiving antiretroviral therapy, 2005 and 2008 (Percentage)

Eastern Asia
2005: 10
2008: 19

CIS
2005: 4
2008: 20

Southern Asia
2005: 7
2008: 31

Northern Africa
2005: 27
2008: 40

Sub-Saharan Africa
2005: 14
2008: 43

Latin America & the Caribbean
2005: 46
2008: 54

South-Eastern Asia and Oceania
2005: 28
2008: 57

Developing regions
2005: 16
2008: 42

■ 2005
■ 2008

The 3 by 5 initiative—a global effort to provide 3 million people in low- and middle-income countries with antiretroviral therapy by 2005—was launched in 2003. At the time, an estimated 400,000 people were receiving this life-prolonging treatment. Five years later, by December 2008, that figure had increased 10-fold—to approximately 4 million people— an increase of over 1 million people from the previous year alone. The greatest gains were seen in sub-Saharan Africa, where two thirds of those needing treatment live. By the end of 2008, an estimated 2.9 million people in sub-Saharan Africa were receiving antiretroviral therapy, compared to about 2.1 million in 2007—an increase of 39 per cent.

However, for every two individuals who start treatment each year, five people are newly infected with HIV. The rate of new infections continues to outstrip the expansion of treatment, drawing attention to the urgent need to intensify both prevention and treatment measures.

In 2008, 42 per cent of the 8.8 million people needing treatment for HIV in low- and middle-income countries received it, compared to 33 per cent in 2007. This means that 5.5 million people in need did not have access to the necessary medications. Prompted by new scientific evidence, the World Health Organization revised its treatment guidelines in 2009, which will increase even further the number of people requiring antiretroviral therapy.

Data from 90 low- and middle-income countries show that adult women have a slight advantage over adult men in accessing treatment: about 45 per cent of women and 37 per cent of men in need were receiving antiretroviral drugs by the end of 2008. During that year, about 275,700 children, or 38 per cent of those in need in these countries received treatment. Despite limited availability, approximately 2.9 million deaths have been averted because of antiretroviral drugs.

Expanded treatment for HIV-positive women also safeguards their newborns

More than 90 per cent of the 2.1 million children living with HIV were infected while in the womb, around the time of birth or through breastfeeding. However, this percentage can be substantially reduced by treating an expectant mother with antiretroviral therapy. Over the past decade, the international community has continually committed to scaling up access to health services and reducing the burden of HIV among women and children. These efforts are yielding results. In 2008, 45 per cent of HIV-positive pregnant women, or 628,000 out of 1.4 million, received treatment in 149 low and middle-income countries—an increase of 10 per cent over the previous year.

TARGET
Have halted by 2015 and begun to reverse the incidence of malaria and other major diseases

Half the world's population is at risk of malaria, and an estimated 243 million cases led to nearly 863,000 deaths in 2008. Of these, 767,000 (89 per cent) occurred in Africa.

Sustained malaria control is central to achieving many of the MDGs, and available data show significant progress in scaling up prevention and treatment efforts. Major increases in funding and attention to malaria have accelerated the delivery of critical interventions by reducing bottlenecks in the production, procurement and delivery of key commodities. Countries have also been quicker to adopt more effective strategies, such as the use of artemisinin-based combination therapies and diagnostics to better target treatment.

Production of insecticide-treated mosquito nets soars

Global production of long-lasting insecticidal bed nets, 2004-2009 (Millions)

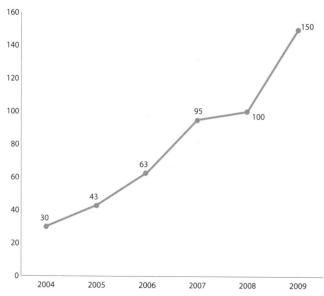

Note: Data for 2007-2009 are based on estimated production capacity.

Global production of mosquito nets has increased fivefold since 2004—rising from 30 million to 150 million in 2009. Nearly 200 million nets were delivered to African countries by manufacturers during 2007-2009 and are available for use; nearly 350 million are needed to achieve universal coverage there. Based on these estimates, endemic African countries have received enough nets to cover more than half of their populations at risk of malaria.

Across Africa, expanded use of insecticide-treated bed nets is protecting communities from malaria

Proportion of children under five sleeping under insecticide-treated bed nets, selected countries, 2000 and 2008/2009 (Percentage)

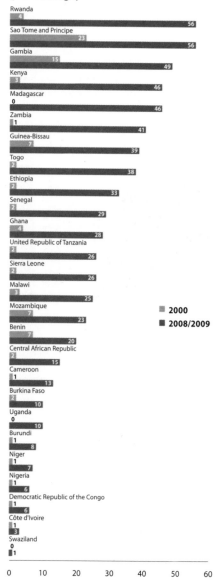

African children, who are among the most vulnerable to malaria, are now sleeping under mosquito nets in far greater proportions than in 2000. All countries with trend data have shown major increases in insecticide-treated bed net use in the last decade, although scaling up in most countries only began in 2005. Across Africa, use of such nets by children rose from just 2 per cent in 2000 to 22 per cent in 2008, in 26 African countries with trend data (covering 71 per cent of the under-five population in Africa). Twenty of these countries documented at least a five-fold increase in coverage during this time, with 11 achieving a 10-fold gain or more.

Poverty continues to limit use of mosquito nets

Children under five sleeping under an insecticide-treated bed net by residence and wealth quintile, sub-Saharan Africa, 2006/2009 (Percentage)

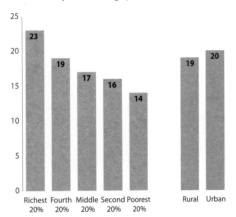

Note: Disaggregation by residence is based on estimates from 32 countries in sub-Saharan Africa with residence information, covering 86 per cent of children under five in the region. Disaggregation by household wealth is based on estimates from 30 countries in sub-Saharan Africa with household wealth information, covering 83 per cent of children under five.

Through campaigns to distribute free insecticide-treated mosquito nets in areas of intense malaria transmission, some countries have been able to achieve more equitable use of bed nets by poor, rural households. But not all countries have managed to do so. On average, girls and boys in the poorest households are still less likely to use mosquito nets, though the data indicate no significant gender differences in use.

Global procurement of more effective antimalarial drugs continues to rise rapidly

Number of doses of artemisinin-based combination therapies procured worldwide, 2001-2009 (Millions)

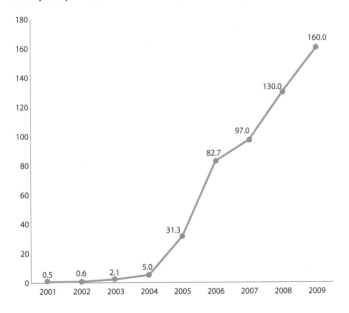

Prompt and effective treatment is critical for preventing life-threatening complications from malaria, particularly in children. In recent years, many African countries have reinvigorated their treatment programmes by increasing access to new combinations of antimalarial medications that have been shown to outperform earlier drugs.

Since 2003, countries have shifted their national drug policies to promote artemisinin-based combination therapies, a more effective—but also more expensive—treatment course. Global procurement of these medicines has risen sharply since 2005.

Antimalarial treatment coverage, however, remains substantially different across African countries—ranging from 67 per cent to only 1 per cent of children under five with fevers receiving any type of antimalarial drug. In fact, the proportion of febrile children under five receiving any antimalarial medication was above 50 per cent in only eight of the 37 African countries with recent data (2005-2009). And in nine of these countries, only 10 per cent or fewer febrile children were receiving treatment. However, lower levels of antimalarial treatment may reflect expanded use of diagnostic tools to only target those children who actually have the disease.

Children from the poorest households are least likely to receive treatment for malaria

Proportion of children aged 0-59 months with fever receiving antimalarial medicines by residence and wealth quintile, sub-Saharan Africa, 2006/2009 (Percentage)

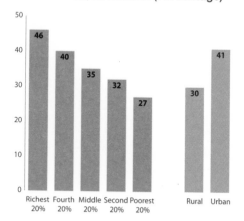

Note: Disaggregation by residence is based on estimates from 33 countries in sub-Saharan Africa with residence information, covering 86 per cent of children under five in the region.
Disaggregation by household wealth is based on estimates from 31 countries in sub-Saharan Africa with household wealth information, covering 83 per cent of children under five.

Children living in rural areas are less likely to receive antimalarial medicines than those living in urban areas. Similarly, children in the richest households are almost twice as likely to receive treatment as those in the poorest households. Data indicate no difference in treatment of girls and boys.

External funding is helping to reduce malaria incidence and deaths, but additional support is needed

Percentage of countries reporting reduction in malaria incidence by funding per person at risk, 108 endemic countries, 2000/2008, (Percentage)

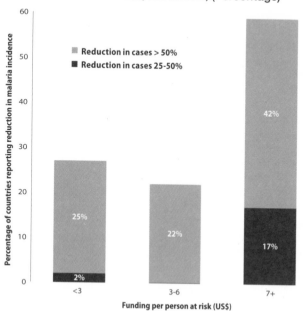

External funding for malaria control has increased significantly in recent years. Funds disbursed to malaria-endemic countries rose from less than $0.1 billion in 2003 to $1.5 billion in 2009. This support came largely from the Global Fund to Fight AIDS, Tuberculosis and Malaria, in addition to more recent commitments from other sources. Domestic contributions are more difficult to quantify, but financing by national governments appears to have at least been maintained at 2004 levels.

Despite these positive trends, total funding for malaria still falls far short of the estimated $6 billion needed in 2010 alone for global implementation of malaria-control interventions. So far, about 80 per cent of external funds have been targeted to the Africa region, which accounts for nearly 90 per cent of global cases and deaths.

Additional funding has resulted in increased procurement of commodities and a larger number of households owning at least one insecticide-treated mosquito net. African countries that have achieved high coverage of their populations in terms of bed nets and treatment programmes have recorded decreases in malaria cases. More than a third of the 108 countries at risk of malaria (nine of them African and 29 non-African) documented reductions in malaria cases of over 50 per cent in 2008, compared to 2000. Although existing data may not be representative of the entire population, decreases in malaria incidence appear to be associated with higher levels of external assistance. This suggests that the MDG target can be reached if adequate funding is secured and key interventions are carried out. Evidence from several African countries also suggests that large reductions in malaria cases and deaths have been mirrored by steep declines in deaths due to all causes among children less than five years of age. Intensive efforts to control malaria could help many African countries reach a two-thirds reduction in child mortality by 2015, as targeted in MDG 4.

One constraint is that the limited funds for malaria control appear to be focused disproportionately on smaller countries, and decreases in incidence are seen primarily in countries with low disease burdens, where gains are more easily achieved. More attention needs to be given to ensuring success in large countries that account for most malaria cases and deaths if the MDG target is to be reached.

Progress on tuberculosis inches forward

Number of new tuberculosis cases per 100,000 population (incidence) and number of tuberculosis case notifications per 100,000 population in the developing regions (including people who are HIV-positive), 1990-2008 (Percentage)

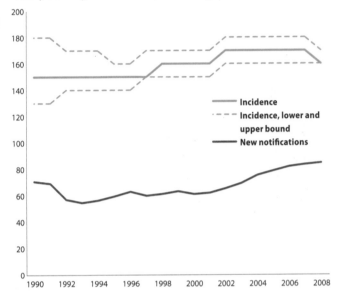

The global burden of tuberculosis is falling slowly. Incidence fell to 139 cases per 100,000 people in 2008, after peaking in 2004 at 143 cases per 100,000. In 2008, an estimated 9.4 million people were newly diagnosed with tuberculosis worldwide. This represents an increase from the 9.3 million cases reported in 2007, since slow reductions in incidence rates per capita continue to be outweighed by increases in population. Of the total number of cases, an estimated 15 per cent are among those who are HIV-positive. If current trends are sustained, the world as a whole will have already achieved the MDG target of halting and reversing the incidence of tuberculosis in 2004.

Tuberculosis prevalence is falling in most regions

Tuberculosis remains the second leading killer after HIV

Number of tuberculosis cases per 100,000 population (prevalence) (including people who are HIV-positive), 1990 and 2008 (Percentage)

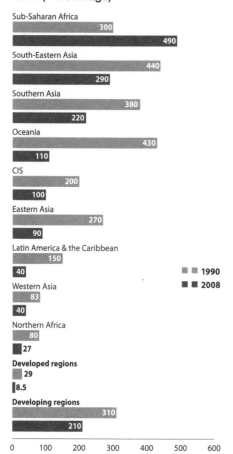

Number of tuberculosis deaths per 100,000 population (excluding people who are HIV-positive), 1990 and 2008

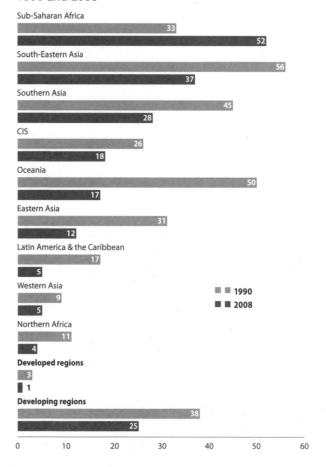

In 2008, tuberculosis prevalence was estimated at 11 million—equivalent to 164 cases per 100,000 people. This is a considerable drop from 2007, which largely reflects a shift in the methodology used in making estimates. Prevalence rates have been falling in all regions except CIS countries in Asia (where, after an initial decrease in the early 1990s, progress has stalled) and in sub-Saharan Africa.

Although more and more tuberculosis patients are being cured, millions will remain ill because they lack access to high-quality care. Tuberculosis remains second only to HIV in the number of people it kills. In 2008, 1.8 million people died from the disease, half of whom were living with HIV. Many of these deaths resulted from the lack of antiretroviral therapy.

Mortality rates from tuberculosis are falling in most regions except CIS countries in Asia, where they appear to be levelling off. In sub-Saharan Africa, mortality rates increased until 2003 and have since fallen, though they have yet to return to the lower levels of the 1990s. Halving mortality by 2015 in that region is highly unlikely due to the negative impact of the HIV epidemic. For the world as whole, reaching the targets established by the Stop TB Partnership—halving the 1990 prevalence and mortality rates by 2015—will be possible only if tuberculosis control efforts and funding for such efforts are sustained.

Goal 7

Ensure environmental sustainability

The rate of deforestation shows signs of decreasing, but is still alarmingly high

Forested area as percentage of land area, 1990 and 2010 (Percentage)

Legend:
- ■ 1990
- ■ 2010

Region	1990	2010
Oceania	68	63
South-Eastern Asia	57	49
Latin America	52	48
Latin America & the Caribbean	52	47
CIS, Europe	48	48
Transition countries of South-Eastern Europe	30	33
Caribbean	26	30
Sub-Saharan Africa	31	28
Eastern Asia	16	20
Southern Asia	14	14
CIS, Asia	4	4
Western Asia	3	3
Northern Africa	1	1
Developing regions	31	29
Developed regions	30	31
World	32	31

Global deforestation—mainly the conversion of tropical forests to agricultural land—is slowing, but continues at a high rate in many countries. Over the last decade, about 13 million hectares of forest worldwide were converted to other uses or lost through natural causes each year, compared to 16 million hectares per year in the 1990s.

Ambitious tree-planting programmes in several countries, combined with the natural expansion of forests in some regions, have added more than 7 million hectares of new forest annually. As a result, the net loss of forest area over the period 2000-2010 was reduced to 5.2 million hectares per year, down from 8.3 million hectares per year in 1990-2000.

South America and Africa continue to show the largest net losses of forests, at just under 4 million and 3.4 million hectares per year, respectively, over the period 2000–2010. In the developed regions, Australia experienced a large loss, partly due to severe drought and fires since 2000. Asia, on the other hand, registered a net gain of some 2.2 million hectares annually in the last decade, mainly because of large-scale afforestation programmes in China, India and Viet Nam. These three countries have expanded their forest area by a total of nearly 4 million hectares annually in the last five years. However, rapid conversion of forested lands to other uses continued in many other countries in the region.

A decisive response to climate change is urgently needed

Emissions of carbon dioxide (CO_2), 1990 and 2007 (Billions of metric tons)

In 2007, global emissions of carbon dioxide (CO_2) again rose, reaching 30 billion metric tons, an increase of 3.2 per cent from the previous year. This represents a 35 per cent increase above the 1990 level. Per capita emissions remain highest in the developed regions—about 12 metric tons of CO_2 per person per year in 2007, compared to about 3 metric tons on average per person in the developing regions and 0.9 metric tons in sub-Saharan Africa, the lowest regional value. Since 1990, emissions per unit of economic output fell by more than 26 per cent in the developed regions and by about 11 per cent in the developing regions.

Figures for 2008 are expected to show a slight shift in the trend: according to the 2009 edition of the *World Energy Outlook,* published by the International Energy Agency, the rate of growth in global CO_2 emissions is expected to have declined in 2008 as a result of the global financial crisis, and global emissions may even have fallen between 2008 and

53

2009. But the same estimates also suggest that the decline will be short-lived: following economic recovery, the agency predicts, global emissions will soon restart their growth and, under a 'reference scenario', are projected to exceed the 1990 level by about 65 per cent by 2020. Such growth is unsustainable and would further increase the risk of profound and adverse effects on the global climate system.

Strengthening international action on climate change remains relevant and urgent. And the window of opportunity afforded by the short-term dip in emissions should be used to the fullest extent. Last year's negotiations under the UN Framework Convention on Climate Change yielded some results, but much remains to be done in order to formulate and put in place a decisive response to the climate change problem by the international community.

The unparalleled success of the Montreal Protocol shows that action on climate change is within our grasp

Consumption of all ozone-depleting substances (ODSs), 1986-2008 (Thousands of metric tons of ozone-depleting potential) and Montreal Protocol's Multilateral Fund replenishment, 1991-2011 (Millions of US dollars)

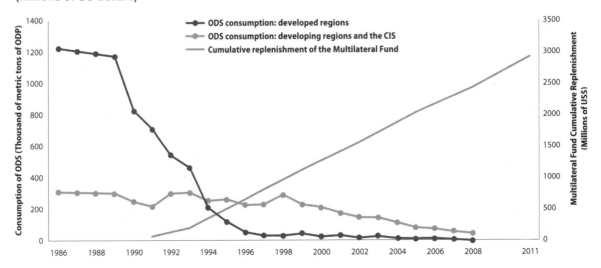

By 16 September 2009, 196 parties had signed the Montreal Protocol, making it the first treaty of any kind to achieve universal ratification. All the world's governments are now legally obligated to phase out ozone-depleting substances (ODSs) under the schedules defined by the Protocol. This year—2010—marks the beginning of a world virtually free of the most widely used ODSs, including chlorofluorocarbons and halons.

Throughout the process, developing countries have demonstrated that, with the right kind of assistance, they are willing, ready and able to become full partners in global efforts to protect the environment. In fact, many

developing countries have exceeded the reduction targets for phasing out ODSs, with the support of the Montreal Protocol Multilateral Fund.

Between 1986 and 2008, global consumption of ODSs was reduced by 98 per cent. Furthermore, from 1990 to 2010, the Montreal Protocol's control measures on production and consumption of such substances will have reduced greenhouse gas emissions by the equivalent of 135 gigatons of CO_2. This is equivalent to 11 gigatons a year, four to five times the reductions targeted in the first commitment period of the Kyoto Protocol, the agreement linked to the UN Framework Convention on Climate Change. Parties to the Montreal Protocol are now examining ways to use the treaty's vigorous implementation regime to promote even greater climate change benefits.

ps

Without the action prompted by the Montreal Protocol and its Vienna Convention, atmospheric levels of ozone-depleting substances would grow 10-fold by 2050. The resulting exposure to the sun's ultraviolet radiation would likely have led to up to 20 million additional cases of skin cancer and 130 million more cases of eye cataracts; it would also have caused damage to human immune systems, wildlife and agriculture. For much of the world, the time it takes to get sunburned would have been dramatically reduced, due to a 500-per cent increase in DNA-damaging ultraviolet radiation.

Reduce biodiversity loss, achieving, by 2010, a significant reduction in the rate of loss

The world has missed the 2010 target for biodiversity conservation, with potentially grave consequences

Though some success in biodiversity conservation has been achieved, and the situation may well have been worse without the 2010 target, the loss of biodiversity continues—unrelentingly. Nearly 17,000 species of plants and animals are known to be threatened with extinction. Based on current trends, the loss of species will continue throughout this century, with increasing risk of dramatic shifts in ecosystems and erosion of benefits for society. Despite increased investment in conservation planning and action, the major drivers of biodiversity loss—including high rates of consumption, habitat loss, invasive species, pollution and climate change—are not yet being sufficiently addressed.

Biodiversity is vitally important for human well-being since it underpins a wide range of ecosystem services on which life depends. Billions of people, including many of the poorest, rely directly on diverse species of plants and animals for their livelihoods and often for their very survival. The irreparable loss of biodiversity will also hamper efforts to meet other MDGs, especially those related to poverty, hunger and health, by increasing the vulnerability of the poor and reducing their options for development.

Key habitats for threatened species are not being adequately protected

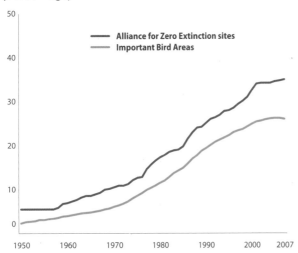

Proportion of key biodiversity areas protected, 1950-2007 (Percentage)

Legend:
— Alliance for Zero Extinction sites
— Important Bird Areas

Note: Data refer to 10,993 Important Bird Areas (IBAs) and 561 Alliance for Zero Extinction sites (AZEs).

Although nearly 12 per cent of the planet's land area and nearly 1 per cent of its sea area are currently under protection, other areas critical to the earth's biodiversity are not yet adequately safeguarded. In 2009, only half of the world's 821 terrestrial ecoregions—large areas with characteristic combinations of habitats, species, soils and landforms—had more than 10 per cent of their area protected. Under the Convention on Biological Diversity, one tenth of the areas of all these ecoregions should have been under protection by 2010.

Progress in key areas of biodiversity has been made, but not fast enough. By 2007, 35 per cent of 561 Alliance for Zero Extinction sites and 26 per cent of 10,993 Important Bird Areas were completely protected, a significant increase from 25 per cent and 19 per cent, respectively, in 1990. Alliance for Zero Extinction sites are home to over 95 per cent of the world population of a 'critically endangered' or 'endangered' species, as defined by the International Union for Conservation of Nature's (IUCN's) Red List of Threatened Species. Important Bird Areas are critical sites for the conservation of the world's birds. Protecting all of these areas would significantly contribute to the Convention on Biological Diversity's target to safeguard areas of particular importance. However, at present, more than two thirds of these sites are unprotected or only partially protected. In addition, while certain areas may be officially 'protected', this does not mean that they are adequately managed or that the coverage provided is sufficient to effectively conserve critical habitats and species.

The number of species facing extinction is growing by the day, especially in developing countries

Proportion of species expected to remain extant in the near future in the absence of additional conservation action (IUCN Red List Index of species survival for birds, 1988-2008, and mammals, 1996-2008)

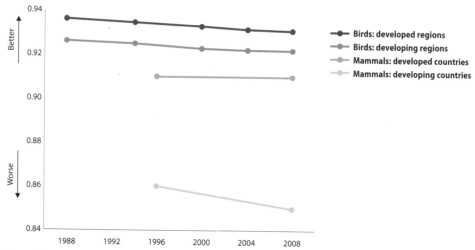

Note: A Red List Index value of 1.0 means that all species are categorized as of 'least concern', and hence none are expected to go extinct in the near future. A value of zero indicates that all species have gone extinct.

The IUCN's Red List Index—which charts the proportion of species expected to remain in existence in the near future in the absence of additional conservation action—shows that more species are being driven towards extinction than are improving in status. Mammals are more threatened than birds. And for both groups, species in the developing regions are more threatened and deteriorating as fast as, or faster than, species in the developed regions.

Overexploitation of global fisheries has stabilized, but steep challenges remain to ensure their sustainability

Global production of marine capture fisheries peaked in 1997 at 88.4 million metric tons and has since declined slightly, to about 83.5 million metric tons in 2006. The proportion of overexploited, depleted and recovering stocks has remained relatively stable over the last 10 years, at about 28 per cent. However, the proportion of underexploited and moderately exploited stocks has declined continuously, indicating that the negative impact of fisheries is increasing. Only about 20 per cent of fish stocks were moderately exploited or underexploited, with the possibility of producing more.

The world is on track to meet the drinking water target, though much remains to be done in some regions

The most progress was made in Eastern Asia, where access to drinking water improved by almost 30 per cent over the period 1990-2008. Although coverage also expanded in sub-Saharan Africa—by 22 per cent over the same period—it remains very low, with only 60 per cent of the population served. Oceania saw no progress over the nearly 20-year period, and coverage remains very low, at about 50 per cent.

In all regions, progress was made primarily in rural areas. In the developing regions as a whole, drinking water coverage in urban areas, which stood at 94 per cent in 2008, has remained almost unchanged since 1990. At the same time, rural drinking water coverage increased from 60 per cent in 1990 to 76 per cent in 2008, narrowing the gap between rural and urban areas.

Proportion of population using an improved water source, 1990 and 2008 (Percentage)

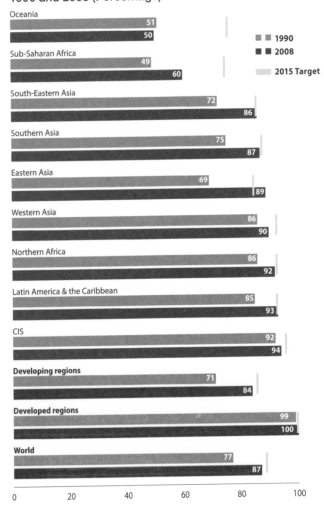

If current trends continue, the world will meet or even exceed the MDG drinking water target by 2015. By that time, an estimated 86 per cent of the population in developing regions will have gained access to improved sources of drinking water. Four regions, Northern Africa, Latin America and the Caribbean, Eastern Asia and South-Eastern Asia, have already met the target.

Accelerated and targeted efforts are needed to bring drinking water to all rural households

Safe water supply remains a challenge in many parts of the world

Proportion of population using an improved water source, rural and urban areas, 2008 (Percentage)

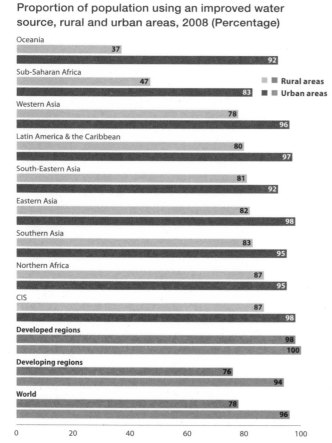

During the last decade, expanded activity in agriculture and manufacturing has not only increased the demand for water, but has also contributed to the pollution of surface and ground water. Moreover, problems of contamination with naturally occurring inorganic arsenic, in particular in Bangladesh and other parts of Southern Asia, or fluoride in a number of countries, including China and India, have affected the safety of water supplies.

In the future, water quality will need to be considered when setting targets for access to safe water. Despite efforts to compile global water quality data, measuring the safety of water can be difficult; in developing regions, it has been attempted so far only in pilot surveys. Rapid, reliable and cost-effective ways of measuring water quality locally and reporting findings at the global level will need to be identified to overcome the current technical and logistic constraints, along with the high cost.

Despite overall progress in drinking water coverage and narrowing of the urban-rural gap, rural areas remain at a disadvantage in all developing regions. The largest disparities are in Oceania and sub-Saharan Africa, but significant differences between urban and rural areas are found even in regions that have achieved relatively high coverage, such as Western Asia and Latin America and the Caribbean.

The rural-urban gap is much wider when only households having a piped drinking water supply on premises are considered. The proportion of people who enjoy the health and economic benefits of piped water is more than twice as high in urban areas than in rural areas—79 per cent versus 34 per cent. Disparities are particularly evident in Oceania and sub-Saharan Africa, where rural coverage of piped water remains very low at 37 per cent and 47 per cent, respectively, as compared to 91 per cent and 83 per cent in urban areas.

Globally, eight out of 10 people who are still without access to an improved drinking water source live in rural areas.

With half the population of developing regions without sanitation, the 2015 target appears to be out of reach

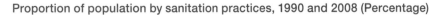

Proportion of population by sanitation practices, 1990 and 2008 (Percentage)

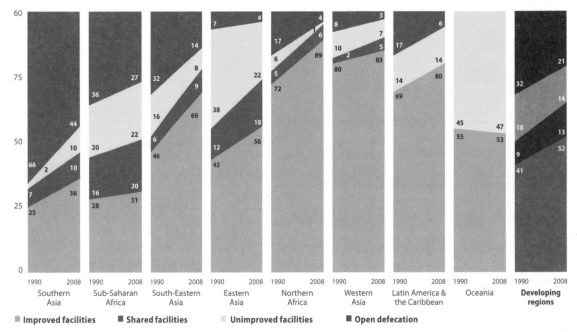

■ **Improved facilities**　　■ **Shared facilities**　　▢ **Unimproved facilities**　　■ **Open defecation**

Note: Data for Latin America & the Caribbean and Oceania are not sufficient to provide regionally representative estimates of the proportion of the population who use shared sanitation facilities.

At the current rate of progress, the world will miss the target of halving the proportion of people without access to basic sanitation. In 2008, an estimated 2.6 billion people around the world lacked access to an improved sanitation facility. If the trend continues, that number will grow to 2.7 billion by 2015.

In 2008, 48 per cent of the population in developing regions were without basic sanitation. The two regions facing the greatest challenges are sub-Saharan Africa and Southern Asia, where 69 per cent and 64 per cent of the population, respectively, lack access.

Among sanitation practices, the one that poses the greatest threat to human health is open defecation. It is encouraging that this practice has declined in all developing regions. However, the largest relative decline was in two regions where open defecation was already practised the least—Northern Africa and Western Asia. In contrast, the least progress (a decrease of 25 per cent) was made in sub-Saharan Africa, where rates of open defecation are high. Southern Asia, which has the highest rate of open defecation in the world (44 per cent of the population), made only limited progress.

The practice of open defecation by 1.1 billion people is an affront to human dignity. Moreover, indiscriminate defecation is the root cause of faecal-oral transmission of disease, which can have lethal consequences for the most vulnerable members of society—young children. If open defecation rates continue to decline, the impact on reducing child deaths could be enormous, primarily by preventing diarrhoeal diseases and the stunting and undernutrition that tend to follow. Success stories among some of the poorest and most disadvantaged groups in society show that behaviours can change. What is required is the political will to mobilize the resources needed to stop open defecation, which represents the greatest obstacle to tackling the sanitation problem.

Disparities in urban and rural sanitation coverage remain daunting

Proportion of population using an improved sanitation facility in urban and rural areas, 2008 (Percentage)

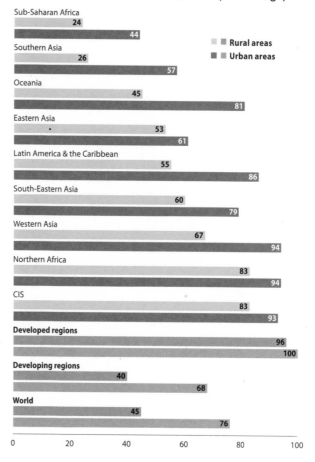

Most progress in sanitation has occurred in rural areas. Over the period 1990-2008, sanitation coverage for the whole of the developing regions increased by only 5 per cent in urban areas and by 43 per cent in rural areas. In Southern Asia, coverage rose from 56 per cent to 57 per cent of the urban population—a mere 1 per cent increase—while doubling in rural areas, from 13 per cent to 26 per cent. The gap between rural and urban areas, however, remains huge, especially in Southern Asia, sub-Saharan Africa and Oceania.

Improvements in sanitation are bypassing the poor

Sanitation practices by wealth quintile, sub-Saharan Africa, 2005/2008

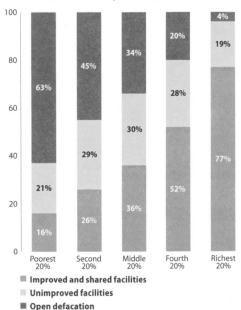

- ■ Improved and shared facilities
- ☐ Unimproved facilities
- ■ Open defacation

An analysis of household surveys conducted during 2005-2008 shows that the richest 20 per cent of the population in sub-Saharan Africa are almost five times more likely to use an improved sanitation facility than the poorest 20 per cent. These same findings show that open defecation is practised by 63 per cent of the population in the poorest quintile and by only 4 per cent of the richest quintile.

Sanitation and drinking water are often relatively low priorities for domestic budget allocations and official development assistance, despite the huge benefits for public health, gender equity, poverty reduction and economic growth. And in many instances, interventions are not targeted to the population most in need.

Slum improvements, though considerable, are failing to keep pace with the growing ranks of the urban poor

Population living in urban slums and proportion of urban population living in slums, developing regions, 1990-2010

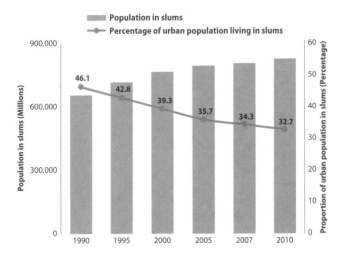

Over the past 10 years, the share of the urban population living in slums in the developing world has declined significantly: from 39 per cent in 2000 to 33 per cent in 2010. On a global scale, this is cause for optimism. The fact that more than 200 million slum dwellers have gained access to either improved water, sanitation or durable and less crowded housing shows that countries and municipal governments have made serious attempts to improve slum conditions, thereby enhancing the prospects of millions of people to escape poverty, disease and illiteracy.

However, in absolute terms, the number of slum dwellers in the developing world is actually growing, and will continue to rise in the near future. The progress made on the slum target has not been sufficient to offset the growth of informal settlements in the developing world, where the number of urban residents living in slum conditions is now estimated at some 828 million, compared to 657 million in 1990 and 767 million in 2000. Redoubled efforts will be needed to improve the lives of the growing numbers of urban poor in cities and metropolises across the developing world.

Moreover, the recent housing crisis, which contributed to the larger financial and economic downturn, may offset the progress that was made since 1990. Although the crisis did not originate in developing regions, it has hit their populations and cities, where millions continue to live in precarious conditions, often characterized by a lack of basic services and serious health threats. In many cases, public authorities have exacerbated the housing crisis through failures on four major counts: lack of land titles and other forms of secure tenure; cutbacks in funds for subsidized housing for the poor; lack of land reserves earmarked for low-income housing; and an inability to intervene in the market to control land and property speculation. Low incomes in the face of rising land prices virtually rule out the possibility that the working poor can ever own land, contributing to the problem of urban slums.

A revised target for slum improvement is needed to spur country-level action

When the international community adopted the Millennium Declaration and endorsed the 'Cities without Slums' target in 2000, experts had underestimated the number of people living in substandard conditions. They had also determined that improving the lives of 100 million slum dwellers was a significant number and a realistic target to be achieved within the next 20 years. Three years later, in 2003, new and improved data sources showed for the first time that 100 million was only a small fraction—about 10 per cent—of the global slum population. In addition, unlike other MDGs, the slum target was not set as a proportion with reference to a specific baseline (generally the year 1990). Instead, the target was set as an absolute number, and for the world as a whole. This makes it difficult, if not impossible, for governments to set meaningful country-specific goals. Clearly, the target will require redefinition if it is to elicit serious commitment from national governments and the donor community— and hold them accountable for continued progress.

Slum prevalence remains high in sub-Saharan Africa and increases in countries affected by conflict

But the situation is even more critical in conflict-affected countries, where the proportion of urban populations living in slums increased from 64 per cent to 77 per cent between 1990 and 2010. The impact of conflict is also reflected in the increased proportion of slum dwellers in Western Asia, largely due to the deterioration of living conditions in Iraq. There, the proportion of urban residents living in slums has more than tripled—from 17 per cent in 2000 (2.9 million people) to an estimated 53 per cent in 2010 (10.7 million people).

Proportion of urban population living in slum areas, 1990 and 2010 (Percentage)

Note: Countries emerging from conflict included in the aggregate figures are: Angola, Cambodia, Central African Republic, Chad, Democratic Republic of the Congo, Guinea-Bissau, Iraq, Lao People's Democratic Republic, Lebanon, Mozambique, Sierra Leone, Somalia and Sudan.

Among developing regions, sub-Saharan Africa is estimated to have the highest prevalence of urban slums, followed by Southern Asia. Less than a third of the populations of other developing regions are living in slums. Despite the efforts of some sub-Saharan African countries and cities to expand basic services and improve urban housing conditions, inaction by others has prevented overall progress from keeping pace with rapidly expanding urban populations.

Goal 8

Develop a global partnership for development

Aid continues to rise despite the financial crisis, but Africa is short-changed

Official development assistance (ODA) from developed countries, 2000-2009 (Constant 2008 United States dollars and current United States dollars)

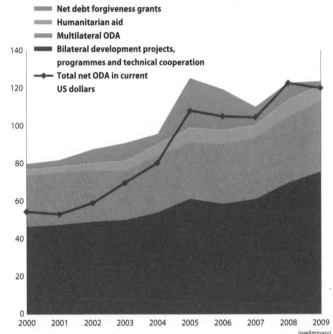

In 2009, net disbursements of official development assistance (ODA) amounted to $119.6 billion, or 0.31 per cent of the combined national income of developed countries. In real terms, this is a slight increase (of 0.7 per cent) compared to 2008 even though, measured in current US dollars, ODA fell by over 2 per cent—from $122.3 billion in 2008.

If debt relief is excluded, the increase in ODA in real terms from 2008 to 2009 was 6.8 per cent. If humanitarian aid is also excluded, bilateral aid rose by 8.5 per cent in real terms, as donors continued to scale up their core development projects and programmes. Most of the increase was in new lending (20.6 per cent), but grants also rose (by 4.6 per cent, excluding debt relief).

At the Gleneagles Group of Eight (G-8) Summit and the UN World Summit in 2005, donors committed to increasing their aid. Many of these pledges were made in terms of a share of gross national income (GNI). Based on expectations of future GNI, these pledges, combined with other commitments, would have lifted total ODA from $80 billion in 2004 to $130 billion in 2010 (at constant 2004 prices). However, the slowdown in economic growth since 2008 has reduced the previously expected level of GNI in the developed countries and the dollar value of the commitments for 2010 to around

$126 billion (at constant 2004 prices). Moreover, the economic slowdown has put pressure on government budgets in the developed countries. While the majority of the initial commitments remain in force, some large donors have reduced or postponed the pledges they made for 2010. On the basis of current 2010 budget proposals, as well as the lower GNI forecasts, total ODA for 2010 is projected to be $108 billion (at 2004 prices).

The shortfall in aid affects Africa in particular. At the 2005 Gleneagles Summit, G-8 members projected that their commitments, combined with those of other donors, would double ODA to Africa by 2010. Preliminary data for 2009 show that bilateral ODA to Africa as a whole rose by 3 per cent in real terms. For sub-Saharan Africa, bilateral aid increased by 5.1 per cent in real terms over 2008. It is estimated that Africa will receive only about $11 billion out of the $25 billion increase envisaged at Gleneagles, due mainly to the underperformance of some European donors who earmark large shares of their aid to Africa.

TARGET
Address the special needs of the least developed countries, landlocked countries and small island developing states

Only five donor countries have reached the UN target for official aid

Net official development assistance from OECD-DAC countries as a proportion of donors' gross national income, 1990-2009 (Percentage)

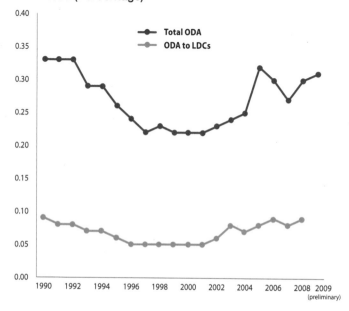

Aid remains well below the United Nations target of 0.7 per cent of gross national income for most donors. In 2009, the only countries to reach or exceed the target were Denmark, Luxembourg, the Netherlands, Norway and Sweden. The largest donors by volume in 2009 were the United States, followed by France, Germany, the United Kingdom and Japan.

This year is a milestone for European Union members of the Development Assistance Committee of the Organisation for Economic Co-operation and Development. In 2005, DAC-EU member states agreed to reach a collective total of 0.56 per cent of GNI in net ODA in 2010, with a minimum country target of 0.51 per cent.

Some countries will achieve or even surpass that goal: Sweden, with the world's highest ODA as a percentage of GNI (1.01 per cent), is followed by Luxembourg (1 per cent), Denmark (0.83 per cent), the Netherlands (0.8 per cent), Belgium (0.7 per cent), the United Kingdom (0.6 per cent),

Finland (0.56 per cent), Ireland (0.52 per cent) and Spain (0.51 per cent).

But others are unlikely to reach the target: ODA as a percentage of GNI is estimated at between 0.44 and 0.48 per cent for France, 0.40 for Germany, 0.37 for Austria, 0.34 for Portugal, 0.21 for Greece, and 0.20 for Italy.

This year is also special for DAC-EU donors because it represents the midpoint between their 2005 commitments and the 2015 target date for meeting the 0.7 per cent GNI target.

Aid concentrates increasingly on the poorest countries, with the least developed countries (LDCs) receiving about a third of donors' total aid flows. In 2007-2008, out of an average total of $71.6 billion of bilateral ODA that was allocated for specific purposes, $15.2 billion focused on achievement of MDG 3—the promotion of gender equality and the empowerment of women.

TARGET
Develop further an open, rule-based, predictable, non-discriminatory trading and financial system

Developing countries gain greater access to the markets of developed countries

Proportion of developed country imports from developing countries and from the least developed countries (LDCs) admitted free of duty and admitted free of duty while their competitors' products were subject to a tariff under MFN (preferential duty free access), 1996-2008 (Percentage)

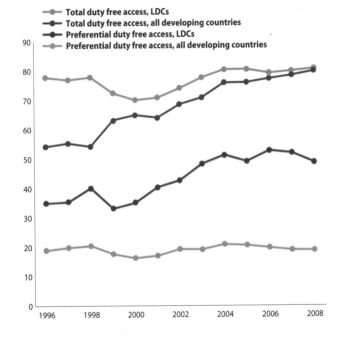

Over the last decade, developing countries and LDCs have gained greater access to the markets of developed countries. The proportion of imports (excluding arms and oil) by developed countries from all developing countries admitted free of duty reached almost 80 per cent in 2008—up from 54 per cent in 1998. For the LDCs, this proportion increased only marginally from 78 per cent in 1998 to almost 81 per cent in 2008.

For the developing countries as a whole, increased market access is attributable mainly to the elimination of tariffs under 'most favoured nation' (MFN) treatment, notably before 2004. Since then, no significant tariff reduction has been made by developed countries in terms of MFN treatment.

Least developed countries benefit most from tariff reductions, especially on their agricultural products

LDCs are 1.6 per cent (versus 8 per cent for other developing countries), though tariffs on clothing and textiles from LDCs are only 2 to 3 percentage points lower than those for developing countries as a group.

Developed countries' average tariffs on imports on key products from developing countries, 1996-2008 (Percentage)

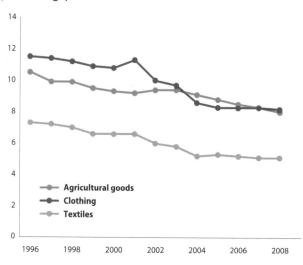

- Agricultural goods
- Clothing
- Textiles

Developed countries' average tariffs on imports on key products from least developed countries (LDCs), 1996-2008 (Percentage)

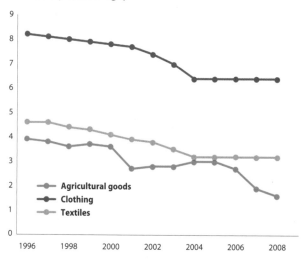

- Agricultural goods
- Clothing
- Textiles

Despite preferences, developed countries' tariffs on imports of agricultural products, textiles and clothing from developing countries remained between 5 per cent and 8 per cent in 2008 and were only 2 to 3 percentage points lower than in 1998. However, least developed countries continue to benefit from larger tariff reductions, especially for their agricultural products. Preferential tariffs on agricultural imports from

Reflecting the advantages over other competitors that preferential tariffs created for LDCs, these countries have increasingly concentrated their exports on products in which they have high preference margins. Further liberalization of the developed countries' trade policies under the Doha Development Agenda would be beneficial for developing countries overall, but it would erode the preferential advantages currently enjoyed by LDCs. However, the preferential treatment granted to LDCs is largely unilateral and the Doha agreement would have the advantage of consolidating these arrangements. In addition, it is expected that preference erosion would be addressed through special implementation procedures within the Doha Development Agenda and through dedicated Aid for Trade.

For the developing countries in general, the main benefits expected from the Doha agreement with respect to access to the markets of developed countries (where most average tariffs are already low) would be the reduction of tariff peaks in agriculture, textile and clothing and the lowering of market-distorting subsidies in agriculture. By reducing high tariffs more than proportionally, the Doha agreement would also decrease the widespread 'escalation' of tariffs (namely the higher tariffs that are applied as the degree of processing of a product increases) that occurs in many instances in both the agriculture and non-agriculture sectors.

In 2008/2009, the financial crisis caused a drop in the value and volume of trade for almost all developing countries. LDCs were especially adversely affected by the drop in the international prices of oil and minerals, their main exports. The value of their oil exports declined by 46 per cent in the fourth quarter of 2008 and continued to drop in early 2009. Despite a recovery in commodity prices starting in the second quarter of 2009, developing countries still suffered a 31 per cent decline in the value of their exports in 2009 (compared to a world average drop of 23 per cent). Faced with this setback, the multilateral trading system played an important role in preventing a widespread retreat into protectionism.

Debt burdens ease for developing countries and remain well below historical levels

External debt service payments as a proportion of export revenues, 2000 and 2008 (Percentage)

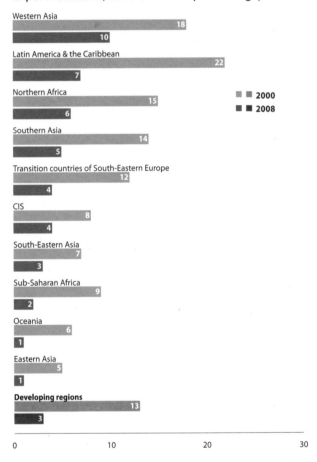

A country's external debt burden affects its creditworthiness and vulnerability to economic shocks. Better debt management, the expansion of trade and, for the poorest countries, substantial debt relief have reduced the burden of debt service. Despite the setback to exports caused by the global economic crisis, the ratio of debt service to exports remained stable or again fell in most developing regions in 2008. Between 2007 and 2008, the ratio increased only in Southern Asia, from 4.8 to 5.4, and in the countries of the CIS, from 3.1 to 3.9. Despite further losses of export earnings in 2009 and, for some countries, declining growth, debt burdens are likely to remain well below historical levels.

Forty countries are eligible for debt relief under the Heavily Indebted Poor Countries (HIPC) initiative. Of these, 35 countries have reached the 'decision point' stage in the process and have had future debt payments reduced by $57 billion; 28 countries that have reached their 'completion point' have received additional assistance of $25 billion under the Multilateral Debt Relief Initiative. The debt burdens of countries included in HIPC initiative are below the average for all least developed countries.

TARGET
In cooperation with the private sector, make available the benefits of new technologies, especially information and communications

Demand grows for information and communications technology

Number of fixed telephone lines, mobile cellular subscriptions and Internet users per 100 population, world, 1990-2009

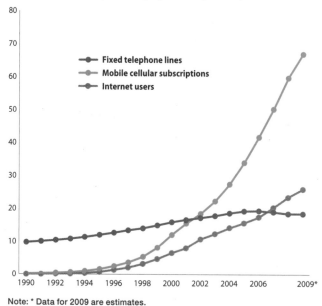

- Fixed telephone lines
- Mobile cellular subscriptions
- Internet users

Note: * Data for 2009 are estimates.

Despite the recent economic downturn, use of information and communications technology (ICT) continues to grow worldwide. By the end of 2009, global subscriptions to mobile cellular services had ballooned to an estimated 4.6 billion—equivalent to one mobile cellular subscription for 67 out of every 100 people. Growth in mobile telephony remains strongest in the developing world, where, by end-2009, mobile penetration had passed the 50 per cent mark.

Mobile telephony is offering new and critical communications opportunities to regions that used to be without access to ICT. In sub-Saharan Africa, for example, a region where fixed telephone line penetration remains at around 1 per cent, mobile penetration has well exceeded 30 per cent. Mobile technology is also increasingly being used for non-voice applications, including text messaging, m-banking and disaster management, and its role as a development tool is widely recognized.

Access to the World Wide Web is still closed to the majority of the world's people

A large gap separates those with high-speed Internet connections, mostly in developed nations, and dial-up users

Number of Internet users per 100 population, 2003 and 2008

Fixed broadband subscriptions per 100 population, 1998-2009, and mobile broadband subscriptions per 100 population, 2000-2009

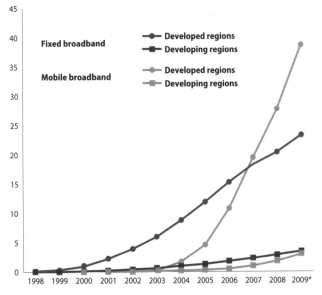

Note: * Data for 2009 are estimates.

Internet use has also continued to expand, albeit at a slower pace over the last year. By the end of 2008, 23 per cent of the world's population (or 1.6 billion people) were using the Internet. In the developed regions, the percentage remains much higher than in the developing world, where only 1 in 6 people are online.

A challenge in bringing more people online in developing countries is the limited availability of broadband networks. Many of the most effective development applications of ICT, such as telemedicine, e-commerce, e-banking and e-government, are only available through a high-speed Internet connection. But a significant divide exists between those who enjoy fast access to an online world increasingly rich in multimedia content and those still struggling with slow, shared dial-up links.

By the end of 2008, fixed broadband penetration in the developing world averaged less than 3 per cent and was heavily concentrated in a few countries. China—the largest fixed broadband market in the world—accounts for about half of the 200 million fixed broadband subscriptions. In most least developed countries, the number of fixed broadband subscriptions is still negligible; service remains prohibitively expensive and inaccessible to most people. However, the introduction of high-speed wireless broadband networks is expected to increase the number of Internet users in developing countries in the near future.

A note to the reader

Measuring progress towards the MDGs

Progress towards the eight Millennium Development Goals is measured through 21 targets and 60 official indicators.[1] This report presents an accounting to date of how far the world has come in meeting the goals using data available as of May 2010.[2]

Most of the MDG targets have a deadline of 2015, and 1990 is the baseline against which progress is gauged. When relevant and available, data for 2000 are also presented, to describe changes since the Millennium Declaration was signed. Country data are aggregated at the subregional and regional levels to show overall advances over time. Although the aggregate figures are a convenient way to track progress, the situation of individual countries within a given region may vary significantly from regional averages. Data for individual countries, along with the composition of all regions and subregions, are available at http://mdgs.un.org.

The basis for this analysis

Regional and subregional figures presented in this report are compiled by members of the United Nations Inter-Agency and Expert Group on MDG Indicators (IAEG). In general, the figures are weighted averages of country data, using the population of reference as a weight. For each indicator, individual agencies were designated as official providers of data and as leaders in developing methodologies for data collection and analysis (see inside front cover for a list of contributing organizations).

Data are typically drawn from official statistics provided by governments. This is accomplished through periodic data collection by ministries and national statistical offices around the world. To fill data gaps, which occur frequently, many of the indicators are supplemented by or derived exclusively from data collected through surveys sponsored and carried out by international agencies. These include many of the health indicators, which are compiled, for the most part, from Multiple Indicator Cluster Surveys (MICS) and Demographic and Health Surveys (DHS).

In some cases, countries may have more recent data that have not yet become available to the relevant specialized agency. In other cases, the responsible international agencies must estimate missing values or make adjustments to national data to ensure international comparability. Data from international sources, therefore, often differ from those available within countries.

The United Nations Statistics Division maintains the official website of the IAEG and its database (http://mdgs.un.org). In an effort to improve transparency, the country data series in the database are given colour codes to indicate whether the figures are estimated or provided by national agencies; they are also accompanied by metadata with a detailed description of how the indicators are produced and of the methodologies used for regional aggregations.

[1] The complete list of goals, targets and indicators is available at mdgs.un.org
[2] Given the time lag between collecting data and analysing them, few indicators can be compiled for the current year. Most of them are based on data from earlier years—generally up to 2008 or 2009.

Reconciling national and international data

Reliable, timely and internationally comparable data on the MDG indicators are crucial for holding the international community to account. They are also important in encouraging public support and funding for development, allocating aid effectively, and comparing progress among regions and across countries. Discrepancies among sources and gaps in national data have raised concerns in the statistical community and troubled country data producers who find themselves dealing with different figures for the same indicator.

A number of initiatives have been launched to reconcile national and international monitoring and to resolve differences in methods and definitions used. These efforts are beginning to yield results. The IAEG has promoted a dialogue between national and international agencies to improve the coherence of national and international data and to ensure the quality and transparency of methodologies and data produced. The IAEG has also provided training on the production of indicators to national statistics experts in more than 40 countries.

Improving monitoring systems

Improved data and monitoring tools are crucial for devising appropriate policies and interventions needed to achieve the MDGs. Although some progress is being made, reliable statistics for monitoring development remain inadequate in many poor countries, and the challenge of building in-country capacity to produce better policy-relevant data is enormous. Since periodic assessment of the MDGs began almost ten years ago, activities have been under way to improve data availability in countries and reporting mechanisms to international organizations. As a result, data production in countries is increasingly aligned with internationally agreed-upon recommendations and standards. Moreover, international agencies have developed a better understanding of countries' data availability and of how to work with national experts to produce and estimate indicators.

More data are now available in the international series for the assessment of trends for all MDGs. In 2009, 118 countries had data for at least two points in time for 16-22 indicators as compared to 2003, when only four countries had the same data coverage. This is the result of increased national capacity to venture into new data collection initiatives as well as to increase the frequency of data collection. For instance, the number of countries with two or more data points on contraceptive prevalence increased from 50 in the period 1986-1994 to 94 in 1995-2004. At the same time, the number of countries with no data on this indicator decreased from 106 to 63. The production of quality data is also expanding in other areas, such as monitoring the spread of HIV, leading to a better understanding of the epidemic. Between 2003 and 2008, 87 developing countries had conducted nationally representative surveys that collected data on comprehensive and correct knowledge of HIV among young women, compared to 48 countries in 1998-2002 and only five prior to 1998. Even in areas with less well-established data collection tools, like the environment, major improvements have been made in obtaining data from national and regional authorities. For example, the number of sites included in the World Database on Protected Areas has increased from just over 1,000 in 1962 to more than 102,000 in 2003 and 134,000 in 2009.

Regional groupings

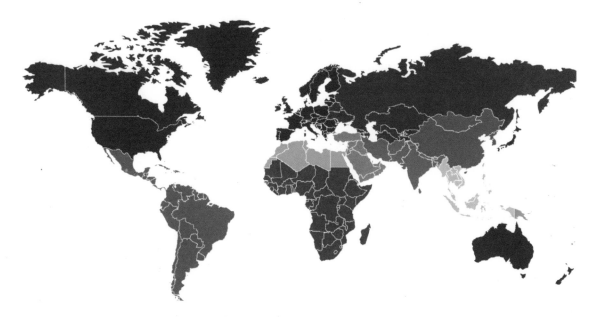

- Developed regions
- Countries of the Commonwealth of Independent States (CIS)
- Northern Africa
- Sub-Saharan Africa
- South-Eastern Asia
- Oceania
- Eastern Asia
- Southern Asia
- Western Asia
- Latin America & the Caribbean

This report presents data on progress towards the Millennium Development Goals for the world as a whole and for various country groupings. These are classified as 'developing' regions, the transition economies of the Commonwealth of Independent States (CIS) in Asia and Europe, and the 'developed' regions.[1] The developing regions are further broken down into the subregions shown on the map above. These regional groupings are based on United Nations geographical divisions, with some modifications necessary to create, to the extent possible, groups of countries for which a meaningful analysis can be carried out. A complete list of countries included in each region and subregion is available at mdgs.un.org.

[1] Since there is no established convention for the designation of 'developed' and 'developing' countries or areas in the United Nations system, this distinction is made for the purposes of statistical analysis only.

The designations employed and the presentation of the material in the present publication do not imply the expression of any opinion whatsoever on the part of the Secretariat of the United Nations concerning the legal status of any country, territory, city or area of its authorities, or concerning the delimitation of its frontiers or boundaries.

For more information visit the UN Statistics Division
Millennium Development Goals website at http://mdgs.un.org

Visit the UN Millennium Development Goals website at
www.un.org/millenniumgoals

Visit the UN Millennium Campaign Office website at
www.endpoverty2015.org

PHOTO CREDITS
Cover: © Sara Duerto Valero
Page 2: © UN Photo/116454
Page 6: © UN Photo/Logan Abassi
Page 11: © Sara Duerto Valero
Page 12: © UNICEF/NYHQ2009-2315/Mosammat Kamrun
Page 15: © UNICEF/NYHQ2009-1732/Truls Brekke
Page 16: © Sara Duerto Valero
Page 19: © UNICEF/NYHQ2009-2314/Mohammad Jashim Uddin
Page 20: © UNICEF/NYHQ1996-1183/Giacomo Pirozzi
Page 21: © Sara Duerto Valero
Page 22: © Sara Duerto Valero
Page 23: © Sara Duerto Valero
Page 26: © UNICEF/NYHQ2006-0038/Brendan Bannon
Page 29: © UNICEF/NYHQ1996-1081/Nicole Toutounji
Page 30: © UNICEF/NYHQ2008-1312/Olivier Asselin
Page 33: © UNICEF/NYHQ2005-1047/Radhika Chalasani
Page 35: © UNICEF/NYHQ2009-2317/Md. Ilias Mia
Page 37: © UNICEF/NYHQ2009-0697/Christine Nesbitt
Page 39: © UNICEF/NYHQ2008-1437/Guillaume Bonn
Page 40: © UNICEF/NYHQ2006-1478/Giacomo Pirozzi
Page 44: © UNICEF/NYHQ2008-0842/John Isaac
Page 46: © UNICEF/NYHQ2010-0402/Kate Holt
Page 52: © Sara Duerto Valero
Page 55: © Sara Duerto Valero
Page 56: © UNICEF/NYHQ2007-0426/Giacomo Pirozzi
Page 60: © UNICEF/NYHQ2009-0859/Shehzad Noorani
Page 63: © UNICEF/NYHQ2009-1449/Peter Wurzel
Page 65: © Sara Duerto Valero
Page 66: © Sara Duerto Valero
Page 69: © Maria Martinho
Page 71: © Masaru Goto / World Bank
Page 73: © Sara Duerto Valero

Editor: Lois Jensen